A History of
The Oakland Stadium
1946-1955

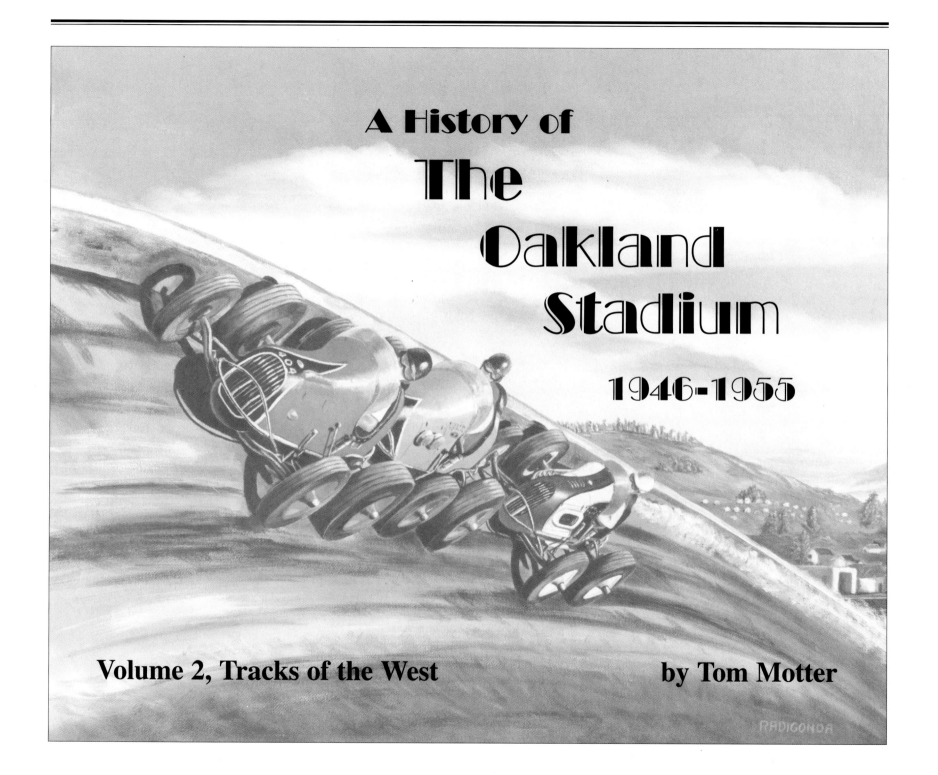

A History of The Oakland Stadium
1946-1955

Volume 2, Tracks of the West

by Tom Motter

Published by

Vintage Images
10042 El Chorlito Drive
Rancho Cordova, CA 95670-3128

Copyright 2001 by
Thomas W. Motter

(All rights reserved)

ISBN 0-9710287-1-0 Hardcover Edition
0-9710287-0-2 Softcover Edition
Library of Congress Control Number 2001089119

Layout and Design by
Rob Motter

Printed in Korea

DEDICATION

A History of
The Oakland Stadium
(1946 – 1955)
Is Dedicated to
David J. (Boots) Archer
A man who embodied the spirit of auto racing in northern
California for over sixty years

FOREWORD

Shortly after the completion of my book *BCRA, The First 50 Years*,[1] it became apparent that the history of automobile racing in northern California was broader than just what had been accomplished by the Bay Cities Racing Association. The history of that midget racing association began in 1938. Its roots went back to 1932; Ken Brenneman played with a small, home-built midget type car that eventually ended up on the track at Hughes Stadium in Sacramento in June 1933. His first outings with the car were at the old one-mile track in San Leandro called the Oakland Speedway, in 1932.

The history of that track[2] tells the story of the history of open wheel racing in northern California. Big cars, stock cars, modified roadsters, midgets, and even motorcycles all raced on that track. It gained a reputation for being one of the fastest in the country.

The legacy of that track is told by the men who raced on it: Louis Meyer, Rajo Jack, Wilbur Shaw and Bud Rose are recalled by any true racing fan now alive. Many of the graduates of that speedway continued their racing careers after World War II at the then newly-constructed Oakland Stadium.

Its high-banked walls soon became legendary, and many of the men who competed at Indianapolis during the 1950s also raced on the Oakland 5/8-mile track. Troy Ruttman and Bob Sweikert, "500" winners, cut their teeth at Oakland, as did many of the men that competed on the A.A.A. (and later, U.S.A.C.) Championship Trail.

Much of racing's recorded history does a good job of telling the stories of such famous high-bank tracks as Winchester, Dayton, Salem, and Ft. Wayne. Almost none of those stories tell about the much higher banks of the Oakland Stadium. I hope that this book corrects those shortcomings.

The projected series, of which this is the second volume, on the history of five western race tracks primarily located in northern California is as follows: Volume 3 will be *A History of the Contra Costa Stadium*, which was located in Walnut Creek, California. Volume 4 will probably be *A History of Capitol Speedway*, long gone from West Sacramento. Finally, Volume 5 will be an essay on *The History of the Airport Speedway (Kearney Bowl)*, a long-time Central Valley favorite located in Fresno, California. If you're wondering how the selection of tracks was made, it's simple: they were favorites of mine.

It took more time than I expected to get the first volume into print, but now that it has seen the light of day, perhaps the others won't be so far behind.

Enjoy!

---

[1] *BCRA, The First 50 Years* by Tom Motter. Published by Bay Cities Racing Association, Pleasant Hill, CA, 1990.
[2] *The History of the Oakland Speedway (1931-1941)*, *Volume 1, Historical Tracks of the West*, by Tom Motter. (In progress) Published by Vintage Images, Rancho Cordova, CA, 2001.

ACKNOWLEDGMENTS

Accumulating material for a book such as this is a monumental job involving many people and sources. Credit for this book goes to all of you; my old friends, family, acquaintances, and new friends.

A history of auto racing is incomplete without photos to help tell the story. The photos in this book (for the most part) are here because of the unselfishness of two people, and special thanks goes to Jim Chini and Randy Reed, both of whom offered their extensive negative collections for inclusion into this book.

My sincere apologies to those whose contributions I have neglected to credit.

Jim Abreu
"Boots" Archer*
Bob Barkhimer
Sammy Belfiore
J. D. Bennett
Bob Burke
Floyd Busby
Jim Chini
Jim Cook
Rod Eschenburg*
Mike Garabedian
Walt Gubanski
Roland Harper
Ray Hiatt
John E. Klann

Jim Lamport
Bayliss Levrett
Lenny Low
Bob Machin
Bill McDonald
Pat Menges
Jeff Millet
Arlene Montgomery
Bill Montgomery
Jim Montgomery
Mary Jane Motter
Rob Motter
Fred Pries
Don Radbruch
Rich Radigonda

Randy Reed
Russ Reed*
Bob Rushing
Alice Scofield
Don Scott
Bob Silva
Jack Staver*
Art Thomas
Ken Urton
Gerald Trueblood
Randy Viglienzone
Dee Walsh
Walter Wiebe

* Gone but not forgotten!

Program cover from the first race held at the Oakland Stadium on June 30, 1946. Big cars, midgets and motorcycle races were run on both the 5/8 and the 1/4-mile tracks.
(Motter Collection)

CONTENTS

Dedication v

Foreword vi

Acknowledgements...vii

Introduction x

Chapter 1: **The Oakland Stadium 1946-1955**..1

Chapter 2: **Big Cars at Oakland Stadium**..11

            The #404 Hisso at Oakland 24

            AAA Sprint Cars on the Oakland 5/8 38

Chapter 3: **Mighty Midgets at Oakland Stadium**..57

            Oakland Racing Star Doubles for Hollywood Film Star 68

            Charles Ashton Curryer 80

Chapter 4: **Stock Car Racing at Oakland Stadium** 97

Chapter 5: **Roaring Roadsters at Oakland Stadium** 137

            All American Soap Box Derby 148

Chapter 6: **Hardtop Racing at Oakland Stadium**..163

            Thrill Show comes to Oakland 174

Chapter 7: **In Conclusion** 187

Index 193

(Motter Collection)

INTRODUCTION
by Bill Montgomery

In 1945, race promoters Bill Linn and Charlie Curryer decided to build a 5/8 and 1/4-mile high banked asphalt speedway.

They selected a sixty-acre parcel of land between San Francisco Bay and the foothills of the Diablo Mountains in San Leandro, California, on the site of the defunct Oakland one-mile dirt track.

During its operation the track hosted roadsters, hardtops, sprint, midget, and stock car races for nine years until it closed its gates to make way for the Bayfair Shopping Center in 1955.

Those are the simple facts that Tom Motter started with when he set out to write the story of the Oakland Stadium.

Tom established himself as a dedicated historian and gifted writer when his first book, *BCRA, the First 50 Years*, was published in 1990.

In this, his latest offering, *The History of the Oakland Stadium*, Tom has used his writing and sleuthing skills to chronicle the history of the Oakland Stadium, sifting through thousands of photos, programs, newspaper clippings, and his own remembrances.

The book is a visual treat, abundantly illustrated with many rare and unpublished photos from the archives of historians, photographers and collectors.

Tom, an accomplished photographer, has spent as much time in the past nine years printing the photos that grace these pages as he did behind the keyboard of his computer writing the manuscript.

Motter also sets the record straight about the debt that is owed to the Oakland Stadium by men like Troy Ruttman, Joe James, Bob Sweikert, and Elmer George, who honed their high bank skills on its daunting banks before becoming AAA Midwest sprint car champions.

I am sure you will enjoy reading Tom Motter's *The History of the Oakland Stadium*.

Bill Montgomery
Fremont, California

Bill Montgomery, author, artist, photographer, and historian in his own right, is the author of the *Official BCRA 1980 Yearbook*, the author/editor of *Distant Thunder*, and he has recently published *Kurtis-Kraft Midget: A Genealogy of Speed*.

THE OAKLAND STADIUM
1946-1955

Russ Reed Photo/Randy Reed Collection

The Oakland Stadium
1946 – 1955

The Search Is On!

In September 1945, just as World War II was ending, Charlie Curryer phoned his old friend and business associate, Bill Linn, to ask what Linn thought about going back into auto racing. Linn thought it was a good idea. The very next day the two of them were flying over the East Bay looking for possible sites for a new race track. They both knew that auto racing could be a big draw after the war, and that there was no time to lose in locating an appropriate piece of property, preferably in the greater Oakland metropolitan area.

Linn had made inquiries about the availability of the land on East 14th Street, site of the old one-mile Oakland Speedway. It was not available because the original owners, the Coelho family, had broken up the property and sub-divided it into about eighty parcels, now belonging to Coelho cousins, uncles, and nephews.

The plan was to purchase enough land on which they could build any kind of an oval track, be it a quarter-mile for midget racing or even a half or a full-mile for big car racing. Even at that time, land prices were becoming prohibitive. At one point, Linn did get an option to buy fifteen acres in back of the Alabam Café at 148th Avenue and East 14th Street, two blocks north of the old Oakland Speedway. The building boom had not yet arrived because of wartime restrictions that had been placed on most building materials, and there were still vacant pieces of property located on East 14th Street in San Leandro. However, finding enough property to build a racing plant on was a real problem. Curryer and Linn considered fifteen acres too small, even for a quarter-mile track, because of parking needs.

That November, Bill Linn was talking with Oakland realtor Foster Weeks. Linn asked Weeks to find him forty or fifty acres for a sports stadium. Weeks suggested property near the Oakland Airport, but Linn believed it to be "too swampy." A suggestion for property near Mt. Eden also was dismissed, because it was "too far away." Weeks suggested that he would try the old speedway site again. This time he managed to obtain an option on the various pieces of property being held by the many members of the Coelho family.

The original Oakland Speedway had been situated on the Coelho property.[1] The site secured by Weeks included 660 feet of frontage on East 14th Street (between 155th Avenue and Plaza Drive), and 1400 feet of frontage on Hesperian Boulevard (between the Western Pacific railroad tracks, halfway between present day Fairmont Drive and Grace Street). Today, the whole sixty-acre parcel (the original Coelho property) is the site of the Bayfair Shopping Plaza.

Deposits were placed on the property on December 10,

---

[1] This piece of property was bounded by Hesperian Blvd. on the West (beginning at about the Western Pacific Railroad tracks which is now the BART track), up to 150th Avenue and East 14th Street, and fronting on East 14th Street on the East and going South from 150th Avenue down to approximately Thrush Avenue, a 60 acre site.

1945, and ground was broken on the new Oakland Stadium on January 15, 1946. Attending the ground-breaking ceremonies were Alameda County Supervisors Harry Bartell and George Janssen, County Engineer Wallace Boggs, William E. (Bill) Linn, President of Oakland Stadium, Thomas Caldecott, Chairman of the Alameda County Board of Supervisors, Charlie Curryer, Vice-President of Oakland Stadium, George Cracknell, manager of the Hayward Chamber of Commerce, Judge A.W. Brunner of San Leandro, Judge Jacob Harder of Hayward, and Sheriff H.P. Gleason of Alameda County.

A New Stadium

The original design of the stadium was figured to cost about $125,000. Many different design changes, which occurred before completion, sent cost estimates to three times the original figure. The final design became more than just an auto race track.

As the word stadium implies, the facility was designed to host a variety of different sporting events. Midgets, stock cars, big cars, and motorcycles were all to have their own racing surfaces. The rest of the facility was supposed to be designed to accommodate a variety of events including football games, rodeos, and other sporting events.

It's evident that midget, big car, roadster, hardtop, and stock car races were held at the Oakland Stadium on a regular basis throughout the life of the track. Original plans called for a 1/5-mile flat dirt track for motorcycle racing, but as it was never built it appears that the intent was for the motorcycles to race on the existing paved surface.

During the month of July 1946, three events were held (two of them on successive Sundays) called "Cavalcade on Wheels." Those afternoon races were made up of a regular midget program concluding with a fifteen-lap main event, a complete big car program ending in a fifteen-lap main event, and a complete motorcycle race culminating in a ten-lap feature event. Motorcycles raced on the same quarter-mile track as the midgets, and therein lay the problem.

As the Class "C" riders (non-sanctioned by the American Motorcycle Association) were used to racing on dirt tracks only, they were skeptical of racing on the paved surface. Consequently, there were only a half-dozen riders competing during the first two "Cavalcade on Wheels" programs.[2] It appears that the motorcycles were not a part of the third portion of the "Cavalcade of Wheels." The motorcycle races were supposed to end with a "Championship Event" to be held on July 28th. There is no evidence that the race ever occurred, and it is assumed that the motorcycles never again appeared at the Oakland Stadium.

As far as is known, there were never any rodeos or football games held at the site, either; however, there were a number of specialty events over the years. In 1946-7-8 the annual All-American Soap Box Derby was held at the track. The Joie Chitwood Thrill Circus performed one-night shows in 1948 and 1949.

The High Banks!

Possibly due to the shape of the property as negotiated by Weeks, that of having the East 14th Street frontage being the nar-

---

[2] Francis Clifford won the first event held on July 4; Dan Hoffman was the winner of the July 7 event. Other riders competing in the two races held were Lou Figone, Ducky Theal, Meeks Hubbard and Bill Crane Jr. Interestingly, these particular riders were not among the "top ranked" riders of the regular Bay Area motorcycle racing scene.

rower side (the Hesperian Blvd. side of the site had almost three times as much frontage), the track was not an exact oval. Aerial photographs plainly show an egg-shaped track as it sits on the property. The straightaways are perpendicular to Hesperian Blvd. and East 14th Street. The larger of the two turns (near Hesperian) was a wide, sweeping turn of about 30 degrees in banking, the tighter turn (near East 14th Street) had a much tighter radius turn with almost 62 degree banking. To accomplish the 62-degree banking, it was necessary to make the foundation of the track (through this turn) thirty feet high.

A True 5/8-mile?

No track in America had turns banked that high![3] The track was built and advertised as being one kilometer or five-eighths of a mile in circumference, measured at its greatest, outside edge, against the outside wall. One reason for the kilometer size was so that the track could be considered in figuring record times in worldwide competition. However, in 1949 Bob Garner, a newspaperman from Redwood City, California wrote to the editor of *Speed Age*[4] *Magazine* questioning whether or not the 5/8-mile Oakland Stadium was truly a 5/8-mile track. Garner reported that he had obtained permission from the track manager, Jim Reed, to actually tape-measure the track.[5] Garner claimed that the track was 337 feet (or 1/16 of a mile) short of being a full 5/8. The management's position that the track was indeed a full 5/8-mile was accepted. Nothing further ever came of the tape measure episode.

Opening Day

Opening day for the Oakland Stadium was set for Sunday, June 30, 1946. Though some construction details were not yet finished, the facility was ready to present race cars to the public. Bill Linn, president of the stadium, and Charlie Curryer, vice president, had anticipated this opening show for months. Then, just two days before the opening, Bill Linn and his family along with Foster Weeks were killed in a small plane crash in the Concord area. It was a sad blow to friends and associates who had seen the two businessmen bring their idea to fruition.

That Sunday afternoon, Freddie Agabashian won the midget show sanctioned by the Bay Cities Racing Association. That the race fans of the Bay Area were pleased could be noted by the fact that the stadium that opening day had attendance in excess of 18,000.

The main grandstand for the stadium was built along the front straightaway (on the north side of the track), and for the opening temporary bleachers were constructed along the back straightaway (on the south side). One month after the grand opening it was announced that the temporary bleachers were to be torn down to make way for permanent grandstands. It was also announced that the start/finish line would be moved to the front (north) straightaway until the new stands could be erected. During most of the track's operation, the start/finish line remained on the front straightaway; however, there were occasions when that line was moved over to the back stretch.

The track when completed was indeed unique. As Curryer

---

[3] Even the dreaded high banks of "The Hills" of Winchester, Salem, Dayton and Fort Wayne never exceeded 38 degrees.
[4] *Speed Age Magazine*, January 1949, Pg. 8
[5] With his 50-foot tape, Garner actually measured the track, foot by foot, using the "fat" part of the track; up against the wall. When he finished, his calculations showed that the track actually measured 2,963 feet in circumference, not 3,300 feet that the 5/8-mile should have been.

and Linn had promised, it really was "The Nation's Most Scientifically Designed Sports Stadium Presenting Outstanding Sporting Events." With the help of Stanford University physicists, consulting engineers, and experienced big-name racing stars, the track would become the second fastest race course in the country,[6] with only the two-and-a-half mile track at Indianapolis having races run at higher speeds than could be accomplished at Oakland.

With the end of the usefulness of the track, it was torn down in 1955. Curryer and Linn had been absolutely correct: its design had indeed been one of the safest in the country.[7] Even though there had been two fatalities at the stadium (two pitmen, in separate accidents) no race driver ever lost his life while running at the Oakland Stadium.

---

[6] Even though the high-banked tracks of Salem, Winchester, Dayton and Ft. Wayne were considered fast, the highest speeds attained at those tracks never exceeded 97mph. In 1955, Jerry Hoyt turned Ft. Wayne's 5/8-mile track in 23.015 seconds (97.38 mph) and at Dayton's ½ mile he turned 19.725 seconds (91.25 mph). In July, 1955, Andy Linden set fast time at Salem's ½-mile track at 20.145 seconds (89 mph).

[7] Due to the construction of a concrete "lip" extending out from top of the track's wall, it was impossible for a race car to fly off of the course. On three different occasions the cars of Bud Rose, Billy Franks and Bill Sheffler did get up onto the "lip", even breaking out pieces of the lip, but never getting outside of the race course.

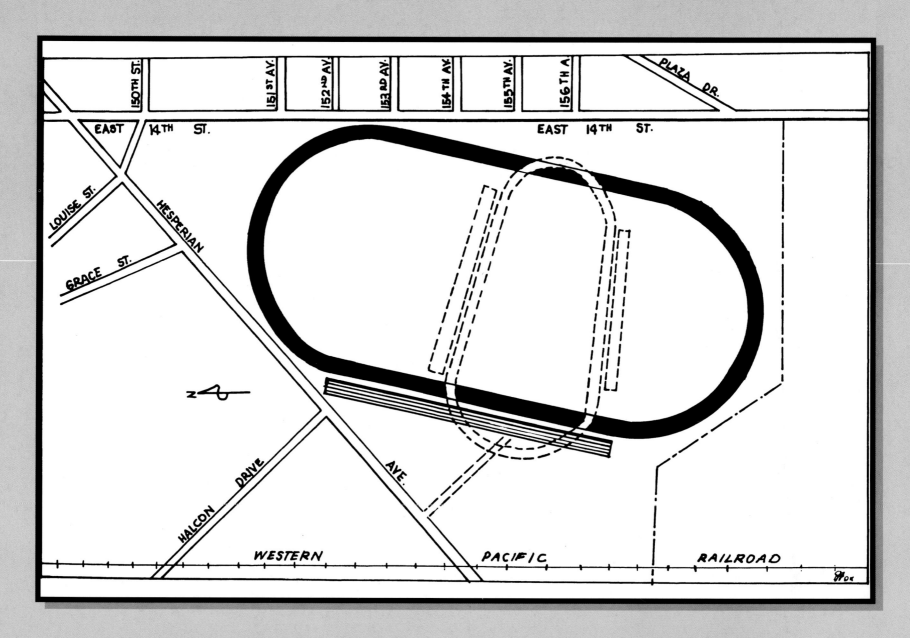

Map of the Oakland Speedway/Oakland Stadium. The one-mile track (solid black), built in 1931, was torn down during World War II. The 5/8-mile track (dotted overlay) was built on the same piece of property in 1946 and demolished in 1955.
(Map drawn by Jack C. Fox, used by permission of Carl Hungness Publishing)

Realtor Foster Weeks, flying his own plane, shot this aerial photo of the future Oakland Stadium in the spring of 1946. Looking south (toward Hayward), East 14th Street is on the left. Hesperian Boulevard is at the bottom. The stadium site is newly graded and the high, 62° bank is taking shape (center, left). The original Oakland Speedway's number-two turn is still visible in lower left of photo.
(*Photo courtesy of The Oakland Tribune*)

Groundbreaking ceremonies for the Oakland Stadium took place on January 15, 1946. Turning the first shovels' full of dirt are, left to right: William E. Linn, President, Oakland Stadium; George Janssen, Alameda County Supervisor; Charles Curryer, Vice President, Oakland Stadium; H.P. Gleason, Sheriff, Alameda County; Judge A.W. Brunner, San Leandro; and Judge Jacob Harder, Hayward.
(Photo courtesy of The Oakland Tribune)

The Oakland Stadium construction is nearly finished in this early June 1946 photo. The 5/8-mile track has been paved but the 1/4-mile portion has yet to be laid down. You're looking at the front straightaway (on left) with the number one turn in the foreground. That's the "flat turn", only 32° banking at this end.
(Photo courtesy of The Oakland Tribune)

Aerial view of the Oakland Stadium taken October 1953. Hesperian Blvd. is at top of photo, East 14th Street runs diagonally through center of photo. The light-colored triangular shapes at top of photo are the Stadium Auto Movie and the Oakland Drive-In theaters.
(Bob Rushing Collection)

BIG CAR RACING AT OAKLAND

Russ Reed Photo/Motter Collection

BIG CAR RACING AT OAKLAND

Sprint Car or Big Car?

As had been the case at the pre-war one-mile Oakland Speedway, sprint cars would hold a special place in the hearts of race fans at the newly constructed Oakland Stadium. Confusion reigns, even today, about the correct nomenclature for the type of racing cars that were bigger than midgets yet smaller than those cars raced at Indianapolis.

Back in 1931, the Indy facility had been built specifically to showcase the very same cars that were running the American Automobile Association's (A.A.A.) Championship Trail. Oakland was to be one more stop on the circuit that also included the Indianapolis 500 race held annually on Memorial Day. Races in 1931 were advertised as being for "championship cars," that is, those that raced in the Championship Series. By 1935, the races were referred to as being for "the Indianapolis two-man cars, piloted by the same stars that have written auto racing history at Indianapolis." In '35, two-man cars were the rule at Indianapolis.

After the A.A.A. pullout of racing on the West Coast in 1936, Charlie Curryer stepped into the fray with his own brand of "big car" racing. His group, the American Racing Association (A.R.A.) was running cars that were generally considered class "B" racers; not quite as big nor as powerful or as "nice" as those run by the A.A.A. Curryer's general advertising thrust was to call them "Indy type" or "big cars," and to the general racing fans that was good enough.

I would have to agree with the late Jack Fox, writing in *The Illustrated History of Sprint Car Racing*[1], that the term "sprint car" as sometimes used to describe the very same race cars, had not been in general use before World War II. The term "sprint" was generally used to describe a race of less than 100 miles. During the Oakland Stadium's early years (1946-47), the ads for races at that track usually made reference to "big car races," and the term stayed in general use for the life of that track with the exception of those times when the A.A.A. came to town and brought with them their brand of big cars. The American Automobile Association called them "sprint cars." By 1960 the term was in general use.

With the opening of the new track in 1946 Curryer had at his disposal a ready group of cars, and drivers eager to bring out their pre-war equipment and go racing. The cars were old, the tires skinny[2], and the drivers sat very high without much protection. Most of the engines powering those old cars were still holdovers from the 1930s. Every variation of the four-cylinder, Model A Ford engine was there. Racing accessories for that engine abounded, with names such as Rajo, Riley (two and four-port), Cragar, D.O.H.C. Frontys, S.O. McDowell Ford T, and

---

[1] Jack C. Fox, *The Illustrated History of Sprint Car Racing* (Speedway, IN: Carl Hungness Publishing, 1985).
[2] Cars brought out to race in 1946 still had their pre-war tires. No new tires were available due to the war effort, and races during the '46 season usually were short events in an effort to preserve tires.

D.O. Fronty Ford T.

It didn't take long before a few of the "hot dogs" from southern California began to bring some of the West Coast's "better" cars north. Bud Rose and his famous No. 3 Rose-Miller, and Bayliss Levrett with his powerful Hisso #404 soon began to give the local boys some competition. Later in the '46 season Bill Sheffler and Hal Cole arrived on the scene with their powerful Offys[3]. Bayliss Levrett, driving his Hisso, was the season-ending champion, with Rose running a close second.

Lenny and the Wall

By this time the venerable Fred Frame[4] had talked a young driver, Lenny Low, into running his car up on the highest portion of the wall. It was Fred's contention that even though this was the "long" way around the track, it would be the fastest. He was right, and for most of that first season Lenny had the "high wall" mostly to himself.

During the 1947 season Hal Cole brought the record lap time down to 23.01 seconds, but by the end of the season Bill Sheffler turned a lap of 22.35 seconds for the astounding average speed of 100.06 mph. This lap time held up until the last race of the 1948 season when Earl Motter, in a midget, lowered the track record to 20.40 seconds.

The big cars at Oakland, under the guidance of Curryer, became a regular Sunday afternoon attraction on the big 5/8-mile track. In 1947 the Bay Cities Racing Association's midget group staged a "strike" in a dispute over the size of the purse that Curryer was paying. The midgets had been running on Tuesday nights on the quarter mile track, and under the lights which illuminated the flat quarter and the high-banked east turn. Curryer let them walk and decided that he could run his big cars on Tuesday nights as well as on Sunday afternoons. It was necessary to provide lighting on the rest of the track since the big cars used the whole five-eighth mile when running. Unfortunately, in order to get the lights up in a hurry (so as not to lose a Tuesday night race) he came up with the idea of stringing wires completely around the track.

The lights, a round-spot type generally used to light a specific area, were 300 watts in power. The effect upon the track at night was one of throwing a "spot" of light, then a distance of darkness, then a "spot" of light again followed by a distance of darkness around the whole perimeter of the track. From the grandstands it was like watching an old time movie with the film out of synchronization. Imagine what it was like for the drivers! The fans didn't like it, and it wasn't too long before the midgets were back running on Tuesday nights and the big cars went back to Sunday afternoons.

A.A.A. and Troy Ruttman

On April 2, 1950, the American Automobile Association (A.A.A.) sanctioned a race on the five-eighths track advertised as a "sprint car" race. In actuality, they were the same cars that Curryer had been running, with the addition of some of the better A.A.A. cars showing up for the race. Some of the better talent of the day included Troy Ruttman in the #2 Malloy Offy, Johnny Mantz in the Agajanian #98jr Offy, Bob Sweikert in the

---

[3] By season's end, Hal Cole held the 5/8-mile track record (also a world's record) at 25.53 seconds (95.6 mph).

[4] Fred Frame, 1932 Indy "500" winner, had become associated with Charlie Curryer and the Oakland Speedway in the mid-1930s. Frame's official position at the Oakland Stadium was Chief Steward.

Karl Orr car, Andy Linden in the Morales Offy, and Duane Carter in the Conze Offy. The rest of the field was filled in with members and cars from the American Racing Association.

When qualifying was over Troy Ruttman had out-qualified eighteen of the top drivers in the nation with a time of 19.24 seconds (116.89 mph), setting the all-time 5/8-mile track record at the Oakland Stadium, a record never broken![5]

The line-up for the fifty-lap main event, called the "Oakland Stadium Sweepstakes," was open to the twelve fastest qualifiers. Ruttman, the top qualifier, had his choice of front row position and chose to start on the outside of the first row. Among those in the main event field were eight existing and future Indy 500 drivers, including Andy Linden, Duane Carter, Cal Niday, Troy Ruttman, Dempsey Wilson, Bud Sennett, Jim Rigsby, and Johnny Mantz. Of those eight, Ruttman went on to win the 500 Classic at Indianapolis in 1952. Bob Sweikert won it in 1955.

1952

The next time the A.A.A. came to race at Oakland, on February 10, 1952, the promoters billed the race as the "Pacific Coast Big Car Races" and not as "sprint car" races as they had two years earlier. They were the same cars and drivers that had participated in the April 1950 event, but they were now called "big cars." This time Ruttman was driving the Agajanian 98jr car[6], and Duane Carter was in the Malloy Offy.

Qualifying and race times were slower than those of the 1950 event. For the 1952 race a broken white line had been painted on the track surface below the high-banked wall. Additionally, just to make sure that the drivers didn't get up on the higher portion of the track, hay bales were placed up on the wall next to the white line. All of this was done just to make sure that the drivers didn't get up on the higher portion of the track, the fastest way around.

To drivers like Ruttman, who were used to running up on the top, it was a frustrating day not to be able to run flat-out. A photograph from that day shows Ruttman hitting one of the bales and throwing hay all over the track. It was no accident that Ruttman hit the bales, just his way of showing the officials what he thought of their intentions!

Ruttman, fastest qualifier of the day at 23.74 seconds, won the fifty-lap main event followed by Jim Rigsby, Joe James, Bob Scott, and Duane Carter in that order.

Big car racing at Oakland continued through 1953 and 1954, although the number of races was cut back because of reduced fan interest. Again, the problem with the cars running on the full 5/8-mile was they were beginning to look like "parade laps," single-file affairs with little or no passing.

When the track's management decided to fill in the banked turns with dirt and thereby eliminate the "rim-riding," it was too late. The crowds were gone, and more importantly so was the track. There were a few more big car races held in 1954 on the dirt/asphalt combination track, but they weren't well attended.

Thus ended big car racing in Oakland.

---

[5] This event was run on the full 5/8-mile track, up against the "high wall." Ruttman's sprint car was powered with a 220 cu. in. Offenhauser engine, almost twice the size of the 136 cu. in. Ford engine that Bob Veith used in setting the midget mark of 20.11 seconds (112 mph) the previous year.

[6] Ruttman had teamed up with J.C. Agajanian early in the year. That May, driving the Agajanian #98 champ car, he won the '52 Indy "500."

Billy Franks crashes in 1946. Notice chunks broken out of wall at top of the track. No race car ever got over the wall and out of the track at Oakland. Franks was unhurt and drove another car later that day.
(Russ Reed Photo/Motter Collection)

Lenny Low in the Dobry Hal #69 in 1946. This was Lenny's regular ride during the '46 season.
(Lenny Low Collection)

Lenny Low in the Hisso #404 poses for the camera on August 11, 1946. This was Lenny's first ride in the car after its regular driver, Bayliss Levrett, crashed the car in a southern California race.
(Lafayette Photo/Chini Collection)

Red Corbin poses in one of promoter Charlie Curryer's "corporation cars." These were pretty much stock, 6-cylinder Fords with stock running gear. Curryer had six of these cars built to help fill in the field when car counts were low.
(Don Radbruch Collection)

Bud Rose poses in his famous #1 Miller at Oakland.
(Lafayette Photo/Chini Collection)

Al Benoit in Eric Gillson's #9 Special. This car has been restored and is now owned by Marshall Mathews of Palo Alto, California.
(Russ Reed Photo/Chini Collection)

Rajo Jack in his own Miller Marine, 183 cu. in. car. By 1946 this car was getting a bit "tired." *(Don Radbruch Collection)*

Bud Sennett tries out the cockpit of the Karl Orr 220 cu. in. Offy in preparation for a May 1949 W.R.A. sprint car race at Oakland.
(Russ Reed Photo/Chini Collection)

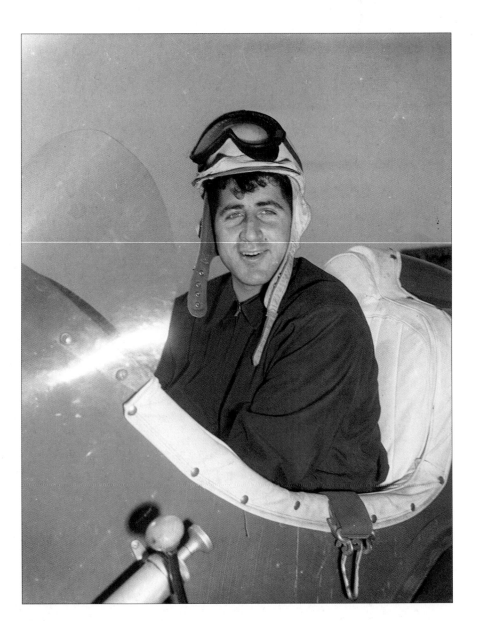

Ted McDonald sits in his own Studebaker Champion-powered sprinter in front of turnstiles at Oakland Stadium in 1952. Car started life in 1946 as a midget, and then was "stretched."
(Bill McDonald Collection)

By February of 1952 Oakland resident Ed Elisian had left the track roadster ranks and was driving sprint cars.
(Russ Reed Photo/Randy Reed Collection)

Joe Gemsa drove many different cars and owned many more. Here he poses in one of the nicest-looking cars he ever had. Notice the copious amounts of chrome!
(Russ Reed Photo/Chini Collection)

The #404 Hisso at Oakland Stadium

The story of the #404 Hisso that raced at Oakland is more a story of the friendship of two men than it is of a race car.

Just when the #404 car was built isn't known. What is known is that the French-designed Hispano-Suiza, a V-8 aircraft engine first built in 1916, was used as power for the SPAD fighter plane. It didn't take long for the Merkler Machine Works, a Fort Wayne, Indiana, engine rebuilding business, to realize that one side of the V-8 could be used as a four-cylinder racing engine. By casting a new crankcase for the engine, along with a lot of other work, they came up with a very powerful racing engine that proved to be a winner during the years prior to World War II.

The car made its first appearance at the Oakland Stadium in 1946 when Bayliss Levrett, a well-known southern California driver who had begun racing in 1933, purchased it from Merkler. The car, with the number 404 on its tail and Bayliss in the cockpit, was soon recognized as one of the cars to beat.

Many race fans have always assumed that the three-digit number (404) was a reference to the engine's cubic inch displacement. This was never the case. The original V-8, in its aircraft configuration, displaced 715+ cubic inches, producing about 150 horsepower. In using only one side of the original 715 cu. in. engine you would have been left with about 358 cu. in. As a matter of record, the Merkler/Levrett Hisso measured 359 cu. in. with a 4¾ inch bore and a 5-inch stroke. It is interesting to note that the Oakland-based American Racing Association (A.R.A.), with whom Levrett raced, had no restrictions on the size of engines for their racing cars.

Bayliss Levrett in the Hisso won the A.R.A. title for 1946, beating out the popular Bud Rose and his Miller by a margin of 31 points.

Lenny Low grew up in Fresno, California. As early as 1936 the fifteen-year-old lad would hitchhike from Fresno to Oakland, just to watch the "big cars" run on the one-mile oiled dirt track. Just prior to the war, in 1941, Lenny built a "big car" for the Oakland track, raced it once, and promptly blew the engine. Before he had a chance to rebuild the car World War II came along, and Lenny enlisted in the Army Air Corps. His discharge, in May of 1946, coincided with the opening of the new 5/8-mile track at Oakland, and he immediately set about getting the race car back together. He installed a six-cylinder Hudson engine in it, painted the number "41" (to signify the year it was built) on the tail, and went racing.

In 1947, at a race at Carrell Speedway in southern California, Bayliss crashed the Hisso badly. The car was almost totally destroyed, and Bayliss wasn't doing too well himself.

Bayless Levrett, owner and driver of the #404 Hisso car, in 1947.
(Lafayette Photo/Chini Collection)

Severe burns on the back of both legs resulted in open wounds that took more than a year to heal. Lenny Low went to southern California, picked up the car, and brought it back to San Leandro, where he parked it in his driveway. Because of the close friendship of the two Bayliss asked if Lenny, with his expert engineering and machine skills, would restore the Hisso.

Once Lenny got the famous #404 back in one piece he became the driver of the car while Bayliss was recovering from his injuries. Lenny was just as successful as Bayliss in the car, and it wasn't long before the owners of Fry's Auto Wreckers in San Leandro approached Bayliss about purchasing the car. An arrangement was made to sell Fry's the car for $4,000, and Lenny continued on as the driver of the Hisso. Bayliss subsequently purchased two Winfield Rocker Arm race cars; one he raced, the other he sold.

By 1950 the Lows were expecting a child, and Betty was asking Len to get out of the racing game. It was after Lenny quit driving the #404 that he finally hung up his helmet and retired from racing. The #404 Hisso, owned by Fry's Auto Wrecking, was eventually turned over to driver Floyd Glidewell.

Following his recuperation Bayliss continued racing at Oakland and elsewhere, and by 1949 he had built and entered his own car in that year's Indy "500." Even though the car went out on the 52nd lap he was awarded "rookie of the year" honors. During practice for the 1952 Indy race, Bayliss crashed the car in what many said was one of the most terrifying crashes seen at the Speedway. Not wearing a seat belt, Levrett was partially tossed out of the car when it hit the wall. While being dragged more than 1000 feet, a fuel line broke spraying him with gasoline, and even though he was able to crawl away from the wreck the resulting fire caused first and second-degree burns on his arms and legs. It was at this point that he decided his racing career was over.

The friendship between the Levrett and Low families, however, was not. In 1970 the Lows left San Leandro, relocating their machine and manufacturing business to Reno, Nevada. The next year Bayliss' son John moved from Glendale to work for Lenny, and one year after that Bayliss moved to Reno where he joined the two at Lenny's shop. Bayliss still lives in Reno near his son John, who operates a transmission repair shop. Lenny has retired from his forklift business, and he and his wife Betty still reside in Reno.

At some point during the years that Floyd Glidewell was driving the #404, a 110 cu. in. Offy was installed in the car. When Fry's ultimately sold the car to a fellow in San Jose it was without engine; however, the Hisso engine went along as a "spare." The Merkler/Hisso engine ended up in the collection of long-time race announcer Jack Carmody. Sometime later #404 was cut up, and none of the original parts now exist.

The two old friends, Bayliss and Lenny, still see each other on a regular basis.

Lenny Low in the cockpit of the Hisso after Bayliss Levrett's 1947 crash.
(Russ Reed Photo/Randy Reed Collection)

Tex Peterson (#23) in the Marsh Baldwin D.O. Cragar, and Bayliss Levrett (#404) in his own Hisso during the 1947 A.R.A./W.R.A. race at Oakland.
(Don Radbruch Collection)

Ed Barnett in the Jack Maurer Offy at Oakland in 1946. Barnett had won the last (1941) 500-miler at the old Oakland one-mile track.
(Don Radbruch Collection)

Trophy girls (and models) almost never get their names mentioned at the races. This pretty lady is Joyce Kincade in a promo photo for the annual 500-lap big car race in 1947.
(Russ Reed Photo/Randy Reed Collection)

Bill Sheffler in his own #1 Offy in 1947. Sheffler held the Oakland 5/8-mile track record until November 1948 when Earl Motter bested it in a midget.
(Don Radbruch Collection)

The personable Bud Rose smiles for his many fans at Oakland. Sure looks like Clark Gable, doesn't he?
(Russ Reed Photo/Chini Collection)

Buck Whitmer in the #1x car about to overtake Jack Menser in the #8. An early 1946 race, the cars were not yet running up on the "highbank."
(Russ Reed Photo/Chini Collection)

Sunday afternoon, July 7, 1946, and Rajo Jack is all through! After hitting a slick spot on the track, Rajo parks it in the wall on the backstretch. Most of Rajo Jack's fame was earned on the pre-war, Oakland one-mile track.
(Russ Reed Photo/Motter Collection)

Another one of Charlie Curryer's "corporation cars." Al Benoit is the driver. Must have been a shortage of cars for the ARA "big car" race that day!
(Don Radbruch Collection)

This car almost defies description! It really is Walt James, and the car really is an old yallar dog! It must have been a brute to drive. *(Lafayette Photo/Chini Collection)*

OAKLAND STADIUM

"World's Finest Speedway"

MAJOR AUTO RACES · MIDGET RACES · MOTORCYCLE RACES · RODEOS · FOOTBALL · BOXING · SPECIAL EVENTS

Charles Curryer, Manager
Cliff D. Allen, Secretary

Main Event Pay Off
May 4 th 1947
including heats

Bud Rose	$880.00
B. Levrett	$704.00
Sennett	$488.00
Tex Peterson	$410.00
Al Morales	$410.00
Geo Gemsa	$322.00
Dobrey-Low	$322.00
Mel Leighton	$264.00
Barnett	$322.00
Buck Whitmer	$264.00
Sheffler	$322.00
Cole	$352.00

B Race total $790.00

Non winners $275.00

Pay-off sheet from an American Racing Association (A.R.A.) big car race at the Oakland Stadium for May 4, 1947. Race promoters paid the money to the car owner, not to the driver.
(Don Radbruch Collection)

Grant Douglas also owned the #B2 car driven by Ed Barnett. This car was powered by a D.O. Hal engine.
(Russ Reed Photo/Chini Collection)

Buck Whitmer in the "Riverside Special," #1X. The car, powered by a D.O. Hal engine and owned by Grant Douglas, was a top performer during the 1946 season.
(Russ Reed Photo/Chini Collection)

By 1949, the famous #404 Hisso had been sold to Fry's Auto Wrecking. Lenny Low was still the driver, but eventually Floyd Glidewell took over the seat. We're not sure if this is Low or Glidewell coming off the high-wall.
(Russ Reed Photo/Chini Collection)

It's impossible to identify the car or the driver, but no mistaking the fact that he's the winner of the event. In 1946 flagmen still officiated from trackside rather than from the safety of a stand above the track surface.
(Russ Reed Photo/Chini Collection)

One of the last sprint car races held at the Oakland Stadium, May 30, 1954. A 250-lapper, starting 33 cars. Notice the turn has been filled in with dirt while the straightaway is still paved. On the outside row are Ernie Miller (#98), Jack Flaherty (#1), Joe Roletto (#2), and Dave Lee (#9). Inside row is unknown, then Don Rossi (#30), unknown, and George Mehalis.
(Russ Reed Photo/Randy Reed Collection)

Bob Frame, son of 1932 Indy winner Fred Frame, poses at Oakland in 1946. Fred Frame worked the Oakland track as an official for Charlie Curryer's A.R.A.
(Russ Reed Photo/Chini Collection)

A.A.A. Sprint Car Auto Races

(This article originally appeared in an Oakland Stadium program dated April 2, 1950. It is presented here just as it was written in 1950. Programs of that time usually did not give credit to authors for articles included in the event program. Since the author is unknown, it is therefore not possible to obtain permission to reprint. We feel it is important to read a "period" piece in its original form, and hope that the original author agrees with us.)

Bits From The Pits

The American Automobile Association boys are back again today to present the second in a series of big time races in the sprint cars over the fastest five-eighths mile course in the nation.

Less than three months ago, on January 15 to be exact, almost the same lineup of cars and drivers made "big time racing" a reality here at Oakland Stadium when they presented the first A.A.A. race in the Bay Area since 1936.

Racing Director Jimmie Reed is sparing no effort and no expense to bring the finest in racing to Oakland Stadium in 1950. A great number of the drivers who are blazing their way 'round the track today, will be among the some 75 of the nation's top throttle stompers who will line up at Indianapolis during the month of May to fight it out in the qualifying runs for positions in the world's greatest sporting event, the 500-mile Memorial Day Classic at the "Brickyard."

Most of the cars racing here today are powered by the internationally famous "Offenhauser" engine, now manufactured in Los Angeles by the Meyer-Drake Engineering Corporation. Different sizes of these engines are made for midgets, big cars and the Indianapolis racers, but they all employ the same engineering design and principles.

Cubic-inch piston displacement for the "Offy" engines here today is 220 c.i. A few cars, notably the No. 4 driven by Bob Sweikert and owned by Karl Orr of Culver City, are powered by Mercury V8 engines converted for racing. Being a "flathead" motor, that is, one with the valves in the block of the engine, a maximum of 299 cubic inch piston displacement is allowed. The Offy has its valves in the cylinder head and that design is considered more efficient than the "flathead" type.

(Left to right) Andy Linden, Duane Carter, and Johnny Mantz, all A.A.A. drivers, at Oakland Stadium on April 2, 1950.
(Russ Reed Photo/Chini Collection)

Under the skilled touch of Karl Orr, the car that Bob Sweikert drives is capable of giving the Offys a real run for the big dough. That fact was revealed last January when Sweikert came in for second place money in the inaugural 50-lap sweepstakes.

Among the drivers here today, the most promising lad and one who is tabbed as a likely winner of the 500-miler this year is young Troy Ruttman of Ontario. One of those "naturals" that pop up once in a decade, Ruttman started in the roadsters three years ago and in his first season became almost invincible in the "rods." Then he stepped into the midgets and quickly became a pilot to be reckoned with. After that, it was but another step to the sprint cars, such as he is driving today and with that experience under his belt he became eligible for the great classic at Indianapolis.

Another great prospect for Indianapolis is the Hayward Flash, "Booming" Bob Sweikert. Displaying capabilities very nearly on a par with Ruttman, he had had similar experience in the past three years and has been a "top hand" at the roadsters, midgets and big cars. Bob is being groomed for a ride at Indianapolis and if present plans go through, he may get that opportunity this year.

A few old friends are now riding under the A.A.A. banner. A great crowd pleaser is the veteran, Art George, of Seattle. George was badly injured in a crackup in the Northwest last summer and was almost six months recuperating. He is now back in action and has been racing down at Carrell Speedway in Gardena. Bud "Scorchy" Sennett, a veteran on the high banks of the five-eighths here, will be driving Marsh Baldwin's fast No. 12 and it is not unlikely that his experience in past triumphs might give him the edge over many of his competitors in today's series of events.

Troy Ruttman (left) in the #2 Malloy Offy and Johnny Mantz (right) in the Agajanian #98jr Offy, race at Oakland on April 2, 1950.
(Sammy Belfiore Collection)

Drivers signal for "one more lap" for the start of the feature in 1947. Bill Sheffler (#1) on the pole, Bud Rose (#3) outside. Second row has Cecil Burnaugh (#14) inside, and Bayliss Levrett (#404) on the outside.
(Russ Reed Photo/Chini Collection)

Al Benoit lines up at Oakland in the #54 Curryer "corporation car."
(Motter Collection)

George Mehalis (#31) and Floyd Glidewell (#404). The #404, after being bought by Fry's Auto Wrecking, still has the Hisso engine in it.
(Russ Reed Photo/Chini Collection)

February 10, 1952. Troy Ruttman in Agajanian's #98jr. shows Oakland officials what he thinks of their idea to run this race down off of the high-wall, below the white line. Hay bales were placed on the white line as a deterrent. Jim Rigsby in Alex Morales' #1 comes through the track where he's supposed to.
(Russ Reed Photo/Chini Collection)

Bayliss Levrett and the #404 Hisso crew pose in the infield at Oakland in 1948. The car and crew never looked better!
(Lafayette Photo/Chini Collection)

Just moments before, Bud Rose (#3) in his own Miller had both front wheels on top of the wall. It appeared that he might go over, but the front-end unhooked and came back down hard, and he was finished for the day. This 1946 action shows Buck Whitmore (#1x) going by. *(Chalmers Davies Photo/Chini Collection)*

Troy Ruttman in the Emmett Malloy Offy after setting the world's record for a single lap on a 5/8-mile course. This record (19.24 seconds/116.89 mph) was set on April 2, 1950 at a A.A.A. sanctioned race at Oakland.
(Russ Reed Photo/Chini Collection)

Although the drivers aren't identified, this photo shows the broken white line painted on the track below the lip of the wall. Promoters did this in an effort to keep the cars from running up on the lip and having the races become nothing more than "parade laps." Banking on this turn was 62 degrees, making Oakland the steepest (and fastest) track in the country.
(Russ Reed Photo/Chini Collection)

Popular driver Lenny Low is being shown the checkered flag held by little Al Vermiel. Al is the brother of Stan and the son of the late Louie Vermiel. This 1950 publicity shot was used on a number of Oakland Stadium programs.
(Russ Reed Photo/Randy Reed Collection)

Cecil Burnaugh (center) is flanked by A.R.A. flagman (left) and Charlie Curryer (right), Oakland promoter and A.R.A. president.
(Russ Reed Photo/Chini Collection)

Duane Carter poses in the Conze Offy. Carter was filling in for Jack McGrath in this April 2, 1950 A.A.A. sprint car race at Oakland.
(Russ Reed Photo/Randy Reed Collection)

Car owner Jack Gaynor hired Dempsey Wilson to drive his 4-port Riley in the April 2, 1950 A.A.A. sprint car race at Oakland. Wilson later appeared at Indianapolis numerous times between 1956 and 1968.
(Lafayette Photo/Chini Collection)

Popular Hal Cole, caught in this 1946 photo at Oakland Stadium, was a pre-war Oakland Speedway favorite. He won the 500-miler held on the one-mile Oakland track in 1940.
(Don Radbruch Collection)

Ernie Miller in the Uptown Motors #98 and Sam Hawks in the Hisso #404 go by a spinning unidentified driver in #23. The high-banked turns had been filled in with dirt for this May 30, 1954 A.R.A. sprint car race.
(Russ Reed Photo/Randy Reed Collection)

Likeable Bob Sweikert in the Karl Orr "K.O. Special." Car was powered by a Mercury flathead V-8. Sweikert was third fastest, and finished 4th in the A.A.A. sprint car race at Oakland on April 2, 1950.
(Lafayette Photo/Chini Collection)

Bayless Levrett posed for the camera in 1946, sitting in his famous #404 Hisso-powered big car. This one-half of a V-8 aircraft engine was a whopping 358 cubic inches.
(Lafayette Photo/Chini Collection)

Johnnie Parsons (in sunglasses) seems to be showing Bob Scott (in car) the fast way to get into the high-banked turn of the Oakland Stadium. Troy Ruttman is obviously telling Parsons to quit giving away all of the secrets. This was a A.A.A. sprint car race held in February 1952. *(Lafayette Photo/Chini Collection)*

There were only three occasions that any race car got close to going over the wall at Oakland. Here #14, driven by Ed Barnett, nearly makes it. Bill Sheffler in #1 barely escapes trouble himself.
(Ernie Lovingood Photo/Chini Collection)

Bob Sweikert in the Karl Orr Mercury Special, and Bud Rose in his own Miller, lead the field down the front stretch for the start of another main event, at the fast 5/8-mile Oakland Stadium in 1949.
(Russ Reed Photo/Motter Collection)

MIDGET RACING AT OAKLAND

Dick Downes-Clay Walsh Collection

MIDGET RACING AT OAKLAND

With four exceptions, all midget races held at the Oakland Stadium between 1946 and 1953 were held on the quarter-mile, paved track formed inside, between the two straightaways utilizing the flat portion of the high-banked number two turn. In those days oval tracks had only two turns; only the Indianapolis Motor Speedway had four turns because it had four straightaway sections.

The owners of the stadium, Curryer and Linn, had envisioned the facility as a track for all types of motor racing. The midgets were always expected to be a big part of that master plan. Indeed, the opening event of the track, on June 30, 1946, was a midget race won by Freddie Agabashian. For the next eleven weeks, on Tuesday nights the mighty midgets held forth on the small, flat 1/4-mile inside the cavernous stadium.

Midget racing was popular at Oakland, as it was everywhere in those early post-war years. The action on the track was fast and furious; the talent displayed was consistent and artful. Since the first turn of the quarter mile track was absolutely flat, lots of maneuvering took place trying to get into that first turn. If the speed was too fast and the driver missed, no problem, he would either continue down the front straight, or at worst, splinter a little bit of timber that made up the crash wall of turn one. Beyond the first turn crash wall was nothing except the flat infield of the rest of the bigger track. Back straightaway speeds were usually a bit higher, due to the fact that the driver entering the second turn (a part of the high bank) could use a bit of the bank to run up on and then slingshot himself down the front straight, being ever mindful of that first, flat, turn one.

1946

During that inaugural first season, Bay Cities Racing Association's mighty midgets appeared at the Oakland Stadium ten times. Out of the ten midget races, Freddie Agabashian won seven of the main events on his way to the BCRA Championship that year. Jerry Piper, Fred Friday, and Bob Barkhimer won the remaining three races of that first season.

1947

A banner year for midget racing in general, 1947 saw BCRA running 159 races during the season. Tuesday nights were reserved for midget racing at the Oakland Stadium, where they raced 21 times that year. Even though Agabashian was the 1947 BCRA driving champion, he only won five events at Oakland. This had nothing to do with Aggie's driving ability; it was just that a much larger contingent of drivers was showing up at the tracks each night. During the '47 season at Oakland, eight different drivers showed up in the winner's circle[1], including

---

[1] Agabashian and Cavanagh won five races each. Smith won four; Holtkamp won two while Brown, Piper and Normi won one each.

Woody Brown, Jerry Piper, Johnny Smith, Frankie Cavanaugh, Johnny Soares, Ed Normi, Norm Holtkamp, and, of course, Freddie Agabashian.

1948

As in the previous year, all races at Oakland were held on the quarter-mile track. Again BCRA had lots of cars, drivers, and tracks to race on. In 1947 BCRA had run 159 races, compared to 151 in 1948. Only six of those races were at the Oakland Stadium. Of the six races held there, five were on the quarter-mile, but the last one, held on November 14, was held on the full, 5/8-mile, high banked oval.

Here, for the first time, midget race fans were treated to the spectacular sight of being able to watch their favorite type of race car and drivers maneuver on this exciting high-banked, high-speed racetrack. The Oakland 5/8-mile track was known nation-wide as one of the fastest tracks in the country, with the Indianapolis Motor Speedway being faster only because it was two and one-half miles in length. The big cars, which had been running at Oakland since its opening in '46, had been using the full track on a regular basis. Crowds were ecstatic about the speeds that were obtained there.

By the time qualifying was over, the fans knew that they were in for an exciting afternoon of midget racing[2]. Earl Motter, driving the Mel Burley V-8/60, had set a new World's record for a single lap on a 5/8-mile track with a time of 20.40 seconds (112 mph). This bettered Bill Sheffler's big car record time by almost two seconds!

Second-fastest time for the day had been set by Bob Sweikert. This set up Motter and Sweikert side-by-side for the rest of the afternoon's events. For the Dash, Motter chose the pole, with Sweikert outside[3]. Sweikert won. For the main event, Motter switched to the outside of the front row, thinking that perhaps Sweikert had found an advantage on the outside. Sweikert started on the inside pole position.

First Lap Crash

Sixteen midgets started the event, straight up according to qualifying times. During the first lap of this main event one of midget racing's most spectacular crashes occurred. As the front of the pack entered the front straightaway, the back of the pack was just entering turn two's high wall. Jimmy Holt went low through the turn, Larry Terra, Eddie Bennett, Woody Brown, Fred Erickson, Johnny Boyd, and Fred Friday all took the high, against-the-wall groove. Within the flick of an eyelash, Holt, Erickson, Brown, Bennett, and Friday were involved in a tangle that had those five race cars strewn about the upper portion of the track. Bennett did several spectacular flips, landing upside-down on the track. Holt, Brown, and Erickson were finished; Terra and Boyd escaped and were able to continue the race. Bennett sustained injuries serious enough to take him to the hospital. Since the field had not successfully completed the first full lap, the race was restarted[4] and went accident-free for the full 35 laps. Sweikert won the 35-lap event, beating Motter in a record time of 13:31.88 seconds, setting yet another World's record!

1949

Midget racing in 1949 was almost as good as in 1948. There were fewer races, although not many. The midget crowds were

---

[2] Twenty one midget pilots had bettered the "Big Car" one-lap record of 22.35 seconds (100.06 mph), set by Bill Sheffler on October 5, 1947.
[3] Fast qualifier had his choice of either the inside or the outside on the front row.
[4] Rules of the day required a complete restart in the event the entire field did not complete the first full lap.

almost as good as the two previous years. Something was beginning to take a bit of the interest away from the mighty midgets. That something turned out to be "hardtops."

There were a total of nine BCRA midget races held at the Oakland Stadium in 1949, and, like the '48 season, all were held on the quarter-mile track except the last race of the season. Again, BCRA's midgets ran the full 5/8-mile, high-banked track on this last race of the year, held on Sunday, November 6, 1949.

Like the previous year, Earl Motter, this time driving the Jack London V-8/60 midget, once again turned in fast time for another new World's record, turning the 5/8-mile in 20.19 seconds. Motter won the trophy dash beating out Johnny Soares, Gene Tessien, and Bob Sweikert. By the finish of the heat races, the rains came down, and the event was cancelled and rescheduled for the next Sunday afternoon.

November 13, 1949, on the 5/8-mile, Bob Veith broke Motter's existing one lap record with a qualifying time of 20.11 seconds, which still stands as the fastest lap ever turned on a 5/8-mile track by a midget[5]. Veith replaced Johnny Soares in the Dash, but other than that it looked like the same line-up as the previous week, differing only in that Veith won the Dash and Motter came in second. The 35-lap feature event looked like a repeat of the previous year, that being Sweikert winning over Motter, again in a record time of 12:39.71 seconds.

Oakland's Last Midget Race

By 1950, the Oakland Stadium was doing more business running hardtop and roadster races than they were with the midgets. Late-model stock cars were popular and the track was beginning to settle into "special events" more than a weekly show. BCRA midgets ran there only once in 1950, twice each in 1951 and '52.

The last appearance of the mighty midgets at the Oakland Stadium occurred on July 19, 1953, for a scheduled 100-lapper on the full 5/8-mile, paved surface. This time there would be a difference in the running on the full track. Because racing on the full 5/8-mile had begun to get boring to the race fans (races up against the wall tended to be "parade laps;" that is, no passing), management decided that they would paint a white line a few feet down from the top, outer-most edge of the track. The white line had the effect of keeping the race cars away from the "line" that was the fastest way around the track. It also had the effect of making the racing a lot more competitive, with more side-by-side action through the corners.

Fast qualifier for this event was Elmer George[6], with a time of 25.33 seconds, much slower than the record times set during the 1948-49 races. This, of course, was due to the fact that the midgets were not running up on "the wall," which was the fastest way around the track. George won the Trophy Dash, with Heat races going to him and Bob Machin. At the start of the scheduled 100-lap Main Event, there was a crash before the completion of the first lap (just as had happened in 1948). The back five cars, driven by Tommy Morrow, Elmer George, Gus Matteucci, Charlie Lawlor, and Norm Lattell came together in a wall-bouncing affair down at the entrance of the first turn. Of those involved in the crash, only Lattell didn't restart the event. At the check-

---

[5] Normally, when a Main Event has to be re-scheduled due to a rainout, the originally qualifying times are used to line up the "make-up" event. The Officials chose to re-run the complete program.

[6] Elmer George was the father of Tony George, the current President of the Indianapolis Motor Speedway and founder of the I.R.L.

ered flag it was Bob Machin driving the number 1 Vic Gotelli car, winning the 100-lap main event[7]. Bill Amans, Bob Ramage, Tommy Morrow, and Earl Motter followed Machin across the finish line, in that order.

Even though this was the last midget race to be run at the Oakland Stadium, there were other types of races run at Oakland during the balance of 1953 and '54.

---

[7] The time for the 100 laps was 44:54.32 seconds, an automatic record for the midgets since this was the only 100 lapper ever run at the track.

These "Midget" midgets, powered by small motorcycle engines, appeared in 1946 as a special event. Five of BCRA's most popular drivers, (L to R) Johnny Smith, Don Smith, Ed Normi, Fred Agabashian and Fred Friday were able to squeeze themselves into these little "mites". *(Lafayette Photo/Chini Collection)*

Eddie Wendt (6) leads Freddie Agabashian (2X) in the opening laps of the very first 12-lap midget main event ever run at the new Oakland Stadium on June 30, 1946. The race was run as an exhibition rather than a scheduled BCRA event. Aggie won the event, followed by Ed Normi, Don Smith, and Eddie Wendt.
(Russ Reed Photo/Motter Collection)

The green flag flies for the start of the first midget race held at the Oakland Stadium, on June 30, 1946.
(Russ Reed Photo/Barkhimer Collection)

Freddie Agabashian in Jack London's #2X. This ex-Ernie Casale/Roy Richter midget won the BCRA championship in 1946 with "Aggie" driving.
(Russ Reed Photo/Chini Collection)

Opening Day, Oakland Stadium, June 30, 1946. These cars are coming off the backstretch, entering turn two (the high one), down low. You can see the abrupt transition between straightaway and turn. The 18,000-plus fans overfilled both the front and back straightaway grandstands.
(Russ Reed Photo/Barkhimer Collection)

Marvin Burke in the Jimmy Massa Continental-powered midget. The "fishtail" was unique in early midget racing.
(Russ Reed Photo/Chini Collection)

Line-up for the main event at Oakland on July 23, 1946. Inside row (front to back): Don Smith, Curly Wells, Buck Whitmer, Ed Normi, Eddie Wendt, and Fred Friday. Outside row (front to back): George Ameral, Johnny Soares, Johnny Smith, Bob Barkhimer, Norm Holtkamp and Fred Agabashian. Agabashian won the 25-lapper.
(Russ Reed Photo/Chini Collection)

Racing Star Doubles for Hollywood Film Star!

Advertising poster for film *To Please a Lady*. Race driver Bud Rose doubled for Clark Gable.
(Motter Collection)

In 1950 Metro-Goldwyn-Mayer film studios released its racing film, *To Please A Lady*, staring Clark Gable and Barbara Stanwyck. It was a typical Hollywood love story that revolved around a race car driver and his passion for racing.

The film had, quite naturally, a large number of authentic racing scenes involving midget, big car, and Indianapolis racing. Inasmuch as Gable was a big-time, high-priced actor in those days, they couldn't afford to have their star being involved in any of the actual racing that was to be a large part of the film.

Enter Bud Rose, a well-known southern California driver. Rose had been a popular racing figure at Oakland, both before and after the war. Particularly, his driving on Oakland Stadium's high banked, 5/8-mile track was well known.

The amazing physical similarity of Rose and Gable made the former a natural as the stand-in double for Gable. All of the racing scenes in the film had Rose handling the driving chores. The close-ups would find Gable sitting in the cockpit. The two looked so much alike that the cameras didn't have to take too many "long-shots" of Rose so that you'd think you were looking at Gable.

Gable had long been considered a sportsman. He was a "man's man," and was often out fishing and hunting when time allowed. The studio oftentimes wondered just what kind of crazy capers their high-priced star was up to. When *To Please a Lady* began shooting, Gable was more than eager to spend time around the races and the drivers. After it was announced that Rose had been selected to be Gable's double, the star made several trips to Oakland just to watch Rose race on the 5/8-mile track. The *Tribune*'s ace photographer, Russ Reed, quick to spot a "local angle," was on hand to record the two together before and after one of those races.

Movie star Clark Gable comes to Oakland to see how real race driver Bud Rose does it.
(Russ Reed Photo/Motter Collection)

Driver Bud Rose sits in midget ready to do a "Take" in scene 47. Action is projected on rear screen. Motorized rollers move tires.
(Motter Collection)

Third heat race action during a day race at Oakland on October 10, 1948. Tommy Cheek (25) in the Cos Cancilla car leads Mike McGreevy (89) in Mel Burley's Ford through the flat first turn on the quarter-mile.
(Russ Reed Photo/Randy Reed Collection)

Billy Ryan poses in his Cos Cancilla ride during the season-ending race held at Oakland on November 13, 1949. Ryan finished sixth in the 35-lap feature held on the full 5/8-mile.
(Lafayette Photo/Chini Collection)

Fred Friday in his own "Speedo-Electric Special" at Oakland Stadium, 1946.
(Russ Reed Photo/Chini Collection)

Cover art sold the excitement of midget racing on early programs. This program was for BCRA's first race on the full 5/8-mile Oakland Stadium track.
(Motter Collection)

Ed Normi (2) started his racing career in 1936 on the Oakland Mile. During WWII he was a B-29 flight instructor. Normi finished second in BCRA points in 1946 in the George Bignotti-owned midget.
(Russ Reed Photo/Chini Collection)

During the running of the second heat race on June 30, 1946, Johnny Soares (18) rode over the wheel of Ed Normi (2), and flipped. Soares was unhurt, while Normi went on to win the event.
(Russ Reed Photo/Motter Collection)

Sixteen-car field parades down the backstretch for the start of the first midget race on the full 5/8-mile Oakland Stadium on November 14, 1948. On the front row are Bob Sweikert in the George Bignotti #7 and Earl Motter in the Mel Burley #89. Sweikert went on to win the 35-lap event.
(Don Scott Photo)

Earl Motter (on the bottom) in the Bob Feehan Drake works hard to get under Marvin Burke (4) in Lenny Gonzel's Ford and Woody Brown (9) in Harry Schilling's Ford. Action at Oakland in October 1948 during the 4th heat race on the quarter-mile track. *(R.Cecconi Photo/Chini Collection)*

This is the main event field asking for "one more lap" before the start of the 35-lap feature on the full 5/8. Sweikert (inside) and Motter (outside) pace the field. November 14, 1948.
(Russ Reed Photo/Motter Collection)

The ever-popular (never quiet) Jack Staver in Fred Friday's #4. Jack finished seventh in the 35-lap feature run on the high-banked, full 5/8-mile track on November 13, 1949.
(Lafayette Photo/Chini Collection)

Charles Ashton Curryer (The Thin Man)

"The Thin Man," Alan Ward, sports editor of the *Oakland Tribune*, called him. Promoter, car owner, track manager, director of racing, and friend of race drivers, describe the man most responsible for much of the auto racing that took place in northern California during the 1930s, 40s and 50s.

Charlie Curryer, director and guiding figure of the American Racing Association (ARA) in southern California, brought his talent for race promotion to northern California in 1932. Some of his first racing promotions were held at the newly built (1928) Sacramento Stadium (later renamed Hughes Stadium), the football and track facility built on the Sacramento Junior College campus in the Capital city of Sacramento.

Motorcycle races, promoted by a local Harley Davidson dealer, were being held on the flat, fifth mile oval laid out around the Junior College football field. Curryer, after seeing several midget car exhibitions at the Oakland Mile track, decided that midget racing on a much shorter track could be a spectator draw. Charlie is credited with organizing the first professional midget races to be held before a paying crowd. On June 3, 1933, at Sacramento Stadium, Curryer persuaded Ken Brenneman and several friends to bring ten of the small racing cars to the first midget race.

Two weeks later Curryer was promoting another midget race in Stockton, California, at the College of the Pacific football field, Baxter Stadium. This was followed immediately by midget races held on the football field of Tracy High School, and soon races were scheduled up and down central California's San Joaquin Valley at various high school sites during the balance of '33. In 1934, Curryer promoted midget races at a defunct dog racing track on Stockton Boulevard in Sacramento, as well as at the Grape Bowl in Lodi, California.

By 1936, when the American Automobile Association (AAA) pulled their racing sanctions out of the Oakland

Top: Curryer (R) presents trophy to Hal Cole (L), winner.
(Russ Reed Photo)

Bottom: Curryer (L) and Joe Gemsa (R) check damage.
(Russ Reed Photo/Chini Collection)

Charlie (The Thin Man) Curryer (r) congratulates Bayless Levrett (l). Levrett was a popular driver at Oakland, and Curryer, the promoter, made sure that his stars were well taken care of.
(Russ Reed Photo/Chini Collection)

Speedway (and the West Coast), Curryer was ready to move his ARA Sprint Car association out of southern California and bring that brand of racing to the fans of northern California. Under Charlie's guidance, open wheel racing at the Oakland plant provided thousands of race fans with exciting racing. Beginning in 1938 and continuing until World War II closed down auto racing throughout the nation, Curryer promoted an annual Labor Day 500-mile "big car" race on that one-mile track, which until modern times were the only 500 mile races ever held outside of the famous "Indianapolis 500."

After the war, Curryer was instrumental in promoting sprint (or big car) races at the newly built 5/8-mile track in San Leandro, as well as promoting a variety of midget races in places like Lodi and Santa Rosa. In 1952 Charlie was the promoter of late model stock car races at Bay Meadows, a one-mile horse racing facility south of San Francisco.

The Oakland Stadium, one of the mainstays for Curryer's racing activities, was torn down in 1955. With its demise Charlie pretty much decided that after three decades of race promoting it was time to "hang it up."

Charlie was always an active participant in his promotions. News photographers could count on his being in any picture when it came time for trophy presentations. He was easy to spot, always wearing either his well-worn fedora or the perennial pith helmet. Most drivers considered Charlie a friend, something not always said about most promoters of the day. When a driver, after having a bad day at one of Curryer's races, was faced with leaving the premises without having won a cent, most often he had a five or ten dollar bill pressed into his hand by Charlie. At least it paid "gas money," and it was usually much appreciated.

Charlie Curryer continued with his ARA until 1959 when it was disbanded, then re-formed by others as the Northern Auto Racing Club (NARC). He passed away in Douglas City, near Redding in northern California, in 1964, and was buried in his hometown of Santa Maria, California.

Earl Motter (89) accepts trophy for setting fast time on Oakland's 5/8-mile. It was a new world's record of 20.40 seconds (112+ mph). *(Greg Sharp Photo/Motter Collection)*

Gene Tessien was a noted track roadster pilot with plenty of experience on the Oakland track. This was one of his few experiences in a midget and he did quite well. This shot, in the Al Dean #10, was in November 1949. Gene qualified fourth fastest for the day, placing him in the 35-lap feature. He finished ninth.
(Lafayette Photo/Chini Collection)

Eli Vukovich (44) came up from Fresno and raced on the Oakland track on a number of occasions. On August 11, 1949 a 100-lapper was held on the quarter-mile track and Eli, driving the Ed Smith Drake, qualified mid-way through the pack and finished second in the semi.
(Jack Fox Photo/Motter Collection)

Eddie Bennett in the Vince Petruzzi "Acme Special" Drake. Bennett did a spectacular flip on the opening lap of the November 1948 race on the high-banked Oakland oval.
(Russ Reed Photo/Randy Reed Collection)

"Fabulous" Freddie Agabashian in George Bignotti's #154. Freddie, a three-time BCRA champion started racing in 1933. He competed in twelve Indy "500" races from 1947 to 1958.
(Russ Reed Photo/Patty Menges Collection)

Buck Whitmer, in Ed Petschaver's #160, started racing motorcycles in 1928. He successfully moved up to "big cars" and was ARA's point champion in 1948. Outside of Buck is Lyle Johnston in Stan Brooks' #5. November 1948.
(Lafayette Photo/Chini Collection)

Earl Motter alongside Mel Burley's fast V-8 after a long day on the high-wall of Oakland. Motter set fast time (20.40 seconds, a new world's record), placed second in the dash, crashed leading his heat race, and finally took a second in the 35-lap feature!
(Greg Sharp Photo/Motter Collection)

Marvin Burke in the Bignotti #154 with Ed Elisian outside in Mel Burley's #14. On the 5/8, November '49.
(Lafayette Photo/Chini Collection)

Chuck Ford in Vic Berado's #61 rail job. This is on the 5/8-mile track, November 1949.
(Lafayette Photo/Chini Collection)

Fred Agabashian in Jack London's #2X adds another trophy to his already bulging display case. 1946.
(Russ Reed Photo/Chini Collection)

Oakland Tribune

July 27, 1947

MIDGET DRIVERS STRIKE, OAKLAND RACES OFF!

Thousands of spectators were told last night in Oakland Stadium there would be no midget auto races because of a strike of the Bay Cities Racing Association, a group of car owners and drivers.

Charles Curryer, manager, declared that only a casual meeting at 5:30 p.m. with D.J. "Boots" Archer, business manager of the association, gave him official information that the drivers would not appear. Curryer declared he was negotiating with the United Racing Association, now appearing each Monday night in Sacramento, to appear at Oakland Stadium next Tuesday. According to Al Slonaker, representing Curryer, the association purses each Tuesday night since June 30 have averaged from $2500 to $3600. Last Tuesday the crowd was thin, and the purse was $1100. The association then demanded a $2500 guarantee and the option of 40 percent. Curryer offered a choice of either the guarantee or the percentage. This was refused, and according to Slonaker, nothing further was heard until he and Curryer walked across the street from the stadium to a restaurant yesterday, where they met Archer, who told them the races were off. Prior to this meeting, the management had assumed that the old agreement of 40 per cent would remain in force while awaiting further negotiations.

Earl Motter (89) and Bob Sweikert (7x) line up for the trophy dash at Oakland on November 14, 1948. Sweikert won the four lap dash in 1m:28.60 seconds, a NTR.
(Lafayette Photo/Chini Collection)

Freddie Agabashian (r) receives his 1948 BCRA championship trophy at Oakland during last race of the season. Presenting trophy is Al Papina, long-time BCRA official.
(Lafayette Photo/Pat Menges Collection)

Johnny Soares (7) makes his move on Mike McGreevy (89) during the main event. Agabashian won, Soares took second, and McGreevy, third. This was a day (10/10/48) race on the quarter-mile.
(R. Cecconi Photo/Chini Collection)

Johnny Smith in the Rudy Hennig (53) car at Oakland on 10/10/48, a day race. Abdo Allen (standing) smiles for the camera. Woody Brown (on the inside) sits in the Harry Schilling #9. Both Smith and Brown failed to finish the 50-lap main.
(Russ Reed Photo/Chini Collection)

A group of aspiring midget drivers take the Eddie Bennett/Jimmy Massa driving school course held at the Oakland Stadium in 1948. Massa (kneeling in front, wearing cap) was a car owner while Bennett (kneeling in front, wearing plaid shirt) was a driver.
(Russ Reed Photo/Chini Collection)

First lap accident at start of first midget race on Oakland's full 5/8-mile track (11/14/48). Jimmy Holt (circle 1) spun in front of Terra (25), Bennett (87), Brown (9), Erickson (36), and Friday (3). All but Terra (25) are gathered up in the tangle, with Bennett flipping three times. *(Rich Cecconi Photo/Motter Collection)*

Bennett (87) is still flipping as Erickson (36), Holt (1), Brown (9), and Friday (3) all try taking evasive action. Johnny Boyd (circle 8) was far enough back that he was able to come down low and avoid all the action. This was the midgets' first time (11/14/48) on the high-banked portion of the full 5/8-mile.
(Russ Reed Photo/Chini Collection)

This is the aftermath of the Bennett flip (previous two photos). Holt is out of his car, Woody Brown is badly shaken, Fred Erickson and Fred Friday are O.K. Eddie Bennett sustains head and shoulder injuries that put him out of action for the next 3-4 months.
(Russ Reed Photo/Chini Collection)

STOCK CAR RACING AT OAKLAND

Russ Reed Photo/Motter Collection

STOCK CAR RACING AT OAKLAND

First of all, the term "Stock Car," as it pertains to the history of the Oakland Stadium, refers to "late model stock cars."

Of all the racing that occurred at the Oakland Stadium, the stock car races seemed to be the most popular. They drew the largest crowds and usually had the largest car counts.

The stadium grandstands situated on both the front and the back straightaways were capable of seating in excess of 18,000 people, and depending upon where the start-finish line was situated, the grandstand in front of the start line was filled first. If it were apparent that an overflow crowd was attending, the second section of grandstands would be opened to accommodate the crowd. At various times, photos taken at most of the stock car races showed full grandstands.

Parade Laps

All stock car races, beginning with the first one held in 1947, were run on the full 5/8-mile, high-banked track. Unfortunately, they took on a "parade lap" appearance. Once the racing cars fell into line, it was usually a follow-the-leader type of event with little or no passing being done because of the peculiar nature of the track. Since the high bank was the fastest way around the track, once the cars were up against that upper wall there was no advantage in dropping down (in the turns) to try to pass another car. The result of that tactic was for a driver to lose his "place" in line, and at that point he could count on watching the "freight train" pass him by. Coming off the high wall at full throttle gave the driver all the speed that could be maintained down the straightaway. Most cars, being "stock," were pretty much evenly matched in terms of speed in those races. Even though the racing wasn't particularly good at this track, it didn't seem to matter to the stock car racing fans, as they continued to come back in droves as soon as the next event was scheduled. What they seemed to enjoy most was the blinding fast speed around the turns and the constant shower of sparks made by the outside sheet metal being ground off against the upper retaining barrier of concrete high up on the top of the track.

Many, if not most, of these cars were near-showroom examples of what was being offered to the American car-buying public at the time, a far cry from the so-called "stock car" racing of today. It was common to see cars on the track that had literally been driven off of a local dealer's showroom or lot. Numbers and dealer identification were painted onto the sides and top of the car, a seat belt was installed along with a strap around the doorpost, and away they went. Most cars ran with full glass in the car, including headlights and windshield wipers. Hubcaps were removed (for faster tire changes), and most cars had hood straps to keep the hoods from flying up in case of front-end damage that might occur during a race.

Sanctioning Bodies

Stock car racing at Oakland was sanctioned, for the most part, by the very same sanctioning bodies that were already racing other types of race cars at the track. The American Racing Association (ARA), primarily running the "big cars" at Oakland, sanctioned a number of late model stock car races on the 5/8-mile track, as did the Western Racing Association (WRA), which was primarily a southern California sprint car racing association. Even Bay Cities Racing Association (BCRA), northern California's premier midget and hardtop group, sanctioned several late model stock car races in the early 1950s.

The sanctioning body, whomever they were, was almost always guaranteed a full contingency of cars and drivers. Entry forms from just their own membership were usually enough to make sure the race had enough local, "name" drivers to attract large crowds of race fans. Those who were considered midget fans would flock to the track to see their favorite midget driver perform in a stock car, as would the big car fans come to see their favorite stars perform in a closed body race car. Invitations sent out of the area to drivers from other associations just helped that much more in assuring large fields of cars and drivers.

Cars and Stars

The very first stock car races were held and sanctioned by the American Racing Association (ARA), headed up by Charlie Curryer. Inasmuch as Curryer was also the vice president of the Oakland Stadium (and its builder) it was natural that he was interested in having this type of racing held at his track. Post-war stock car racing was becoming a real crowd draw. New car models were finally becoming available to the American car buying public by 1947.[1] 1948 brought an even larger increase in new car model production, and by 1949 most every auto manufacturer in Detroit had striking new body styles available. Race fans of this country were more than eager to see these new models on the racetrack. The same fans also delighted in watching a brand-new model car, one that they could hardly afford, being used and abused (crashed!) right in front of their very eyes. Remember that these were truly stock model cars being raced!

Bay Cities Racing Association (BCRA) also ran several very successful stock car races there. Highly regarded midget pilots such as Johnny Soares, Marvin Burke, and Woody Brown were all top performers in the stock car races held at Oakland. Successful midget pilot Johnny Soares, who had started racing before the war[2], won more than his share of stock car titles up and down the state, adding to his stature as an all-around racing driver. Woody (the Boo-King) Brown, BCRA's 1950 midget driving champion, was more popular while driving the stock cars, even more so when his stock car crashed upside-down, which seemed to happen with alarming regularity.

The list of drivers showing up in the stock car racing programs at Oakland in the early 50s included the names of many who would go on to greater fame in open wheel auto racing. Men such as Troy Ruttman, Bob Sweikert, and Roger Ward would go on to become winners at Indianapolis.[3] Johnny Mantz, Ed Elisian, Bud Rose, George Amick, Walt Faulkner, Freddie Agabashian, and Bob Veith are but a few more of the great ones that raced at Oakland.

---

[1] Automobile production was halted during WWII. When the 1946, '47 and even the '48-year model cars were finally brought out they still had the look of the 1942 models, the last model offered before the War.

[2] Soares first raced Modified Street Roadsters with BCRRA in the late 30's. When midget racing continued after the war, he was one of BCRA's top drivers and when BCRA originated its Hardtop Division, Soares was their first Champion.

[3] Ruttman won in '52, Sweikert in '55, and Ward in '59 and '62.

NASCAR Comes to Oakland

On October 14, 1951, big-time stock car racing came to the Oakland Stadium. On this date the National Association of Stock Car Auto Racing (NASCAR) sanctioned a 400-lapper (250 miles) on the big, 5/8-mile track. NASCAR regulars such as Fonty Flock, Dick Rathmann, Allen Heath, and Marvin Panch were in the lineup for Oakland's first Grand National Stock Car Race, right along with local favorites like Woody Brown, Marvin Burke, Bob Caswell, and Johnny Soares. West Coast zone supervisor Johnny Mantz, who had been assigned that post by NASCAR just two weeks before the race, oversaw the event. Driving a 1950 Mercury, BCRA's own Marvin Burke, their 1949 midget driving champ, came in first picking up a winner's check in the amount of $1,875. Bob Caswell, driving a '50 Plymouth, finished second, and Woody Brown (BCRA's 1950 midget champ), driving a 1950 Olds "88," finished third. The race started at least 32 cars, the oldest a '48 Hudson and the newest 1951-year models represented by Oldsmobile, Ford, Plymouth, Studebaker, Nash, Hudson, and even a 1951 model Henry J[4]. It was amazing how many fans were rooting for the Henry J as it ran mostly down on the lower apron of the track. With only a small four-cylinder motor, it wasn't capable of speeds fast enough to run high up in the "groove" with the big boys.

By April of 1952 there had been a total of nine late model stock car races at the Oakland Stadium. A 250-lapper, scheduled for April 6, 1952, would make an even ten events. Mercury and Hudson stock cars had dominated the racing at Oakland, with the Mercs taking five victories and the Hudsons three. An Oldsmobile driven by Woody Brown won one event. BCRA's Marvin Burke accounted for three of the Mercury wins, with Ben Gregory and Dick Meyers accounting for the other two Mercury wins. Bud Sennett, Andy Linden, and Lou Figaro took Hudson victories.

As the 1953 season unfolded it was becoming apparent that stock car racing fans were becoming bored with the cars running on the high banks of the 5/8-mile track. Plainly there wasn't enough passing during these long races, and the numbers at the turnstiles were showing a downward trend that had all the signs of bringing an end to racing at the popular Oakland plant. The hardtop and roadster programs were using mostly the quarter-mile track and they still had enough fans to keep everyone happy. The only midget appearance for 1953 was on the full 5/8-mile and it was deemed a success.

A Premature "Farewell"

In mid-year it became known that the property the track was situated on was about to be sold to a land developer that planned to build a huge shopping center. The printed programs for races held in June and July had announcements that the final races for the big cars and roadsters would be held soon. The July 19th, 100-lap midget race was the "farewell" program for that class of racing.

An announcement placed in the *Oakland Tribune* sports pages in November of 1953 told of a "re-opening" of the Oakland Stadium, with a newly configured track. Apparently the real estate deal had fallen through or at least was put on hold for a while. The "new" track wasn't new at all. What they had done was to fill in the high-banked turns with dirt, thereby leveling out the track. Gone were the high banks that had make Oakland famous, but which had made most of the racing on the walls nothing more than "parades."

---

[4] The Henry J was a low priced, sub-compact model car produced by the Kaiser-Frazer Company, years ahead of the compact cars of the 1970s.

The announcement stated that there would be a Pacific Coast, late model stock car race, to be held on the "New 1/2-mile track"[5]. Interestingly, now the cars would be running down the front and backstretches on pavement and through the turns on dirt. It was a strange combination, to be sure, but it did accommodate a lot more passing, which made for better racing.

NASCAR Returns

After an absence of two years, NASCAR came back to Oakland.

On March 28, 1954 the reconfigured track at Oakland was again the site of a NASCAR "Grand National" race for late model stock cars. This time it was to be 250 laps (125 miles) over the 1/2-mile dirt/asphalt track. Qualifying was done the day before, and by the end of the day twenty-six cars had been entered into Sunday's big race. Fastest of the group was Hershel McGriff, with a qualifying speed of 55.624 mph. All of the West Coast regulars were there, including Woody Brown, Johnny Soares, Clyde Palmer, and Ben Gregory, along with some of NASCAR's "big-guns," such as Marvin Panch and Lee Petty (father of Richard Petty).

Dick Rathmann, winner of ten previous NASCAR Grand Nationals, had been pre-entered but didn't arrive at the track until qualifying had ended and had to start at the very back of the field on race day. McGriff and Marvin Panch led the early stages of the race but at lap 143 Rathmann took his 1952 Hudson Hornet into the lead and stayed there until the checkered flag flew.[6]

Rathmann became the first "last to first" winner in NASCAR Grand National history. Panch, who thrilled the crowd of 8,500 fans with his big broadsides through the dirt corners, finished second, a lap down, while Johnny Soares placed third in his '54 Dodge. Lee Petty, driving the now-familiar number 42, finished sixth, eighteen laps off the pace.

Five months later, on August 1st, NASCAR came back to Oakland for the last time in the track's history. It was a "Grand National" 300-lap (150 miles) race on the 1/2-mile track with the dirt turns and asphalt straightaways. The lineup for the Sunday afternoon race was full of West Coast veteran pilots, including Johnny Soares (who ended up 16th in National points for the year), Woody Brown, Ben Gregory, Clyde Palmer, and Ed Normi. Also included in the lineup for this last NASCAR event at Oakland was Eli Vukovich, brother of Bill Vukovich, winner of the '53 and '54 Indy 500s, along with one of the very few female stock car drivers in the nation, Marian Pagan.

At the finish it was Danny Letner from southern California, driving a '52 Hudson Hornet, narrowly edging out veteran Marvin Panch in his '54 Dodge and thereby gaining his first Grand National victory. Letner and Panch were the only drivers in the field of thirty-three who completed all 300 laps of the race. Following Letner and Panch were Allen Adkins in third, Ben Gregory in fourth, and Lloyd Dane in fifth. Vukovich finished 17th, while Marion Pagan finished 18th.

As it happened, this was to be the last late model stock car race ever held at the Oakland Stadium.

---

[5] The new configuration didn't really change the size of the track at all. With the turns filled in with dirt, cars could not run the outside groove, high up on the wall. The cars would be now be running down closer to the pole, closer to a half-mile distance.

[6] Rathmann's win was even more spectacular owing to an incident that happened prior to the race itself. While towing the Hudson from Chicago to Oakland, the tow vehicle broke down. The racing Hudson had been pressed into service as a tow vehicle and the extra strain on that car weakened the supports for the gas tank. During his qualifying run, the gas tank fell out of the car and was destroyed. Fortunately a previously damaged Hudson, left abandoned in the infield still had a usable tank. It was retrieved, and pressed into service thereby allowing Rathmann to make the race field.

Johnny Soares stands next to his '50 Olds in readiness for an ARA 300-lap race, held 7/27/52, on the 5/8-mile track. Soares won the event.
(Russ Reed Photo/Chini Collection)

Ben Gregory usually placed well in late model stock car races at Oakland. He won a 250-lap race in July '51. This photo shows him at a CSRA/BCRA race at Oakland in 1952.
(Russ Reed Photo/Chini Collection)

Personable Bob Sweikert even found time to race a stock car or two. This 250-lapper was run on 7/16/50 and was won by Marvin Burke. Sweikert, in a '50 Plymouth took a sixth.
(Russ Reed Photo/Randy Reed Collection)

NASCAR sanctioned a 250 lap National race on Oakland's big track on 3/28/54. The turns had been filled in with dirt, cutting the distance of the course from a 5/8-mile to a 1/2-mile. Lee Petty (42) came out west to run this event, finishing sixth. Dick Rathmann won the race from last spot.
(Russ Reed Photo/Motter Collection)

Drivers gather for group photo before the start of a BCRA sanctioned 250-lap race on 7/16/50. Front row includes Ed Elisian, Johnny Smith, Eddie Bennett, Fred Agabashian, Bob Sweikert, and Bob Veith. Back row includes Hershel McGriff, Marvin Burke, Johnny Soares, Walt James, and Woody Brown. Race was won by Marvin Burke in a '50 Mercury before 14,000 fans (an additional 5,000 had been turned away). *(Russ Reed Photo/Chini Collection)*

Late model stock car races drew huge crowds at Oakland's big 5/8-mile track. Here, Fred Steinbroner (16) in a '46 Mercury leads Marvin Burke's (15) '49 Mercury and Johnny Soares in his '49 mercury (2). Burke won the 500-lap race held on 9/25/49, followed by Steinbroner, Hershell McGriff, Bud Rose, and Johnny Key with Elmer George as relief driver.
(Bob Garner Photo/Chini Collection)

Hershel McGriff (3) and Johnny Soares (98) coming off the high-wall at Oakland during 7/52 race. Note how the right-side sheet metal gets scraped from running up against the lip of the banked turn. Soares won the 300-lap race, McGriff finished 5th, nine laps back.
(Russ Reed Photo/Chini Collection)

Marvin Panch (in black jacket) congratulates Danny Letner (w/trophy) upon winning the NASCAR 300-lap race at Oakland on the 1/2–mile. Mel Fernandez (L), official, offers his congrats. Panch took second in the race run on 8/1/54.
(Russ Reed Photo/Chini Collection)

Eddie Bennett (L), Marvin Burke (C), and Walt Faulkner (R) look over the hardware being offered for the BCRA stock car race held on 7/16/50. Burke was the eventual winner.
(Russ Reed Photo/Chini Collection)

Most fans think of George Amick as an AAA/USAC midget and champ car racer. Here is George ready to run a late model stock race on Oakland's 5/8-mile track held on 4/12/53. 11,000 fans watched the 250-lap race won by Marvin Panch.
(Russ Reed Photo/Chini Collection)

The ARA group sanctioned a 250-lap race at Oakland on 10/3/48. Coming off the 62° banked turn are (front to back) Johnny Smith (#46, '48 Ford), Frank Phillips (#27, '48 Ford), Bayliss Levrett (#32, '48 Hudson), Charles Sheppard (#00, '48 Plymouth), Claude Walling (#7, '46 Ford), and Johnny Soares (#9, '49 Mercury). Andy Linden won the race.
(Russ Reed Photo/Motter Collection)

Bob Sweikert (4) leads this group down the backstretch during a 250-lap race on 6/26/49. Sweikert is followed by Fred Steinbroner (16), whose hood had just popped up when photographer Russ Reed caught this shot, George Amick (20), and Bud Rose (3). Stock car races at Oakland always drew crowds in excess of 12,000. Lou Figaro won the race.
(Russ Reed Photo/Chini Collection)

This was the Third Annual Late Model Stock Car race held at the Oakland Stadium, sanctioned by Western Racing Association. Johnny Soares won the race in the pictured Mercury.
(Motter Collection)

Frank Phillips receives winner's trophy for a 1947, 250-mile race sanctioned by ARA. Official Charlie Curryer (R), the promoter, looks on.
(Russ Reed Photo/Chini Collection)

Marvin Panch (fast qualifier) finished second in this 300-lap NASCAR race held on 8/1/54. The turns had been filled in with dirt, the straightaway left as pavement!
(Russ Reed Photo/Chini Collection)

Marvin Panch (R) shows Jim Reed (promoter) what a stock car looks like that runs up against the high-wall of Oakland's 5/8-mile track. Johnny Soares won the 7/27/52 race, followed by Panch and Lou Figaro.
(Russ Reed Photo/Chini Collection)

Ben Gregory, in this straight-off-the-street 1951 Ford, won the 250-lap race on 7/1/51. Johnny Soares (98) was second, followed by Hershel McGriff. Note Gregory's Ford still has headlights, windshield wipers, and license plates!
(Russ Reed Photo/Chini Collection)

Late in 1953 the high-banked turns were filled in with dirt to allow more side-by-side racing through the turns. Here Hershel McGriff (2) gets under Bob Caswell (84) and Marvin Panch (9). This 100-lap, Pacific Coast Championship race was won by Danny Letner followed by Lloyd Dane and Marvin Panch.
(Russ Reed Photo/Chini Collection)

Big car driver Bud Rose poses in his "stock '49 Ford 6-cylinder car. Rose finished 6th in the WRA 250-lap race held on 6/26/49.
(Russ Reed Photo/Chini Collection)

Marvin Burke is awarded the winners trophy from the 7/16/50 BCRA sanctioned 250-lap race. Walt Faulkner placed second, Eddie Bennett took third.
(Russ Reed Photo/Chini Collection)

J.D. Bennett entered his '46 Chevy in the 6/26/49 250-lap stock car race at Oakland. In reality this is 18-year-old Jim Lamport. Not being of legal racing age, Jim borrowed his friend's driver's license and convinced officials he was old enough to drive. He also raced sprint cars and roadsters at Oakland.
(Russ Reed Photo/Chini Collection)

The Hudson Hornet enjoyed several years of success in late model stock car racing. Lou Figaro, posed next to his #33, had his share of that success also. He finished 3rd in this 7/52 ARA sanctioned 300-lap race.
(Russ Reed Photo/Chini Collection)

There was never much passing during these long late model stock car races on Oakland's 5/8-mile. Leading the pack down the front stretch is Danny Weinberg (9) followed by Fred Steinbroner (16), Bob Sweikert (5), and Lou Figaro (33), the eventual winner. Also in the pack are Johnny Soares, J.D. Bennett, George Amick, and Johnny Coates. This was a WRA 250-lap race held on 6/29/49.
(Russ Reed Photo/Chini Collection)

Roger Ward in the '47 Hudson (yes, Ward of "Indy 500" fame) leads Johnny Soares (9) in the 250-lap WRA race at Oakland on 10/3/48. Andy Linden won the race before 15,000 race fans. Soares came in second.
(Russ Reed Photo/Chini Collection)

This group is about to transition from the dirt-filled turns to the asphalt straightaway. In front is Ben Gregory (12). Behind him are Bill Amick (21), Jim Heath (7), and Art Watts (38). Dick Rathmann went on to win this NASCAR 250-lap race held on Oakland's 5/8-mile, now shortened to a half. Rathmann came from last place to win this one on 3/28/54.
(Russ Reed Photo/Chini Collection)

Hershel McGriff (2X) in his 1953 Oldsmobile leads this group down the front straightaway. McGriff went on to win this 500-lap race on 8/2/53.
(Russ Reed Photo/Chini Collection)

8,500 Oakland fans watched as Woody Brown flipped his Mercury stock car during the ARA 300-lap race on 7/27/52. Unhurt, Brown did some hurried repairs and returned to finish 10th. Johnny Soares won the event.
(Russ Reed Photo/Chini Collection)

OAKLAND SPEEDWAY

World's Fastest 5/8 Mile Track

300 LAP STOCK CAR RACE

NASCAR Sanctioned

SUNDAY, AUGUST 1st

OFFICIAL PROGRAM   **25¢**

Program cover from the last Late Model Stock Car race held at the Oakland Stadium on August 1, 1954. NASCAR sanctioned this 300-lap race on the 1/2-mile dirt/asphalt track.
(Jim Montgomery Collection)

Dick Meyer (98) leads Marvin Panch (9) and Hershel McGriff (2X) coming off the high wall at Oakland. McGriff went on to win the 500-lap event (held on 8/2/53) in his '53 Oldsmobile.
(Russ Reed Photo/Chini Collection)

Lou Figaro crashed his #33, '47 Hudson during the running of the WRA sanctioned 250-lapper held on 9/25/49 at Oakland. Marvin Burke won the race.
(Russ Reed Photo/Chini Collection)

Believe it or not, this Henry J (a compact car ahead of its time), with Stan Blaylock driving, finished 7th in the 250-lap late model stock car race held at Oakland on 7/1/51. This group of cars is coming off the 35-degree banked turn, heading down the backstretch.
(Russ Reed Photo/Motter Collection)

Joe Gemsa (6) gets in some practice laps in his Hudson Hornet a few days before a 250-lap race at Oakland on 7/1/51. Ben Gregory won the event, while Gemsa finished 4th.
(Russ Reed Photo/Chini Collection)

Hershel McGriff (9) and Lee Petty (42) lead the pack around for the start of the 250-lap race on the 1/2-mile dirt/asphalt track. There were only three NASCAR late model stock car races at Oakland. Dick Rathmann won this one coming all the way from the back, on 3/28/54. *(Russ Reed Photo/Chini Collection)*

Marvin Panch poses beside his #9 '53 Dodge before the start of a 500-lap race at Oakland on 8/2/53. Hershel McGriff won the event, Panch finished sixth.
(Russ Reed Photo/Chini Collection)

Dick Meyer (with trophy) won the WRA sanctioned 300-lap race held on 6/21/53 at Oakland, followed by Marvin Panch and Woody Brown.
(Russ Reed Photo/Chini Collection)

Joe Gemsa in a pre-race publicity photo for the 7/1/51 250-lapper. He finished 4th. Ben Gregory won it!
(Russ Reed Photo/Chini Collection)

Johnny Soares, at the start of the 6/26/49 WRA 250-lap stock car race at Oakland. Soares won, but after checking the score sheets, Lou Figaro was given the win and Soares given 2nd.
(Russ Reed Photo/Pat Menges Collection)

Claude Walling in his '46 Ford coupe was a noted Pacific Northwest big car driver. He finished 5th in this ARA sanctioned 250-lap late model stock car race at Oakland on 10/3/48.
(Russ Reed Photo/Chini Collection)

This 1949 photo shows cars exiting the number one turn of the Oakland 5/8-mile. This one was banked at "only 35°." The "real" bank, 62°, was at the other end. You think Winchester and Salem were tough? Notice the Crosley running down low. It didn't have enough horsepower/speed to run up against the top of the walls at Oakland.
(Russ Reed Photo/Chini Collection)

Marvin Burke (15) in his '50 Mercury receives the winner's flag at the end of the 250-lap event. Johnny Soares (20) is actually in 5th place. 14,000 fans filled the grandstands while another 5,000 were turned away on this 7/16/50 race.
(Russ Reed Photo/Chini Collection)

Bert Livingston (4) brings his '47 Ford coupe in for water during the ARA sanctioned 250-lap race on 10/3/48. Eventual winner was Andy Linden.
(Russ Reed Photo/Chini Collection)

(Jumpin') Joe Valenti, a popular roadster pilot and BCRA hardtop official, looks over repairs being made to his late model stock car prior to the 8/2/53 500-lap race run at Oakland. Joe finished out of the money.
(Russ Reed Photo/Chini Collection)

Hershel McGriff (L), Jim Heath (C), and Woody Brown (R) before an ARA 250-lap race held on 7/1/51. Ben Gregory won race.
(Russ Reed Photo/Motter Collection)

Hershel McGriff finished 7th in Oakland's 250-lap race held on 7/16/50. 14,000 fans watched Marvin Burke win the event. McGriff was the 1950 Mexican Road Race winner.
(Russ Reed Photo/MotterCollection)

Promoter Charlie Curryer (C) presents Johnny Soares (L) with trophy for winning 300-lap event on 7/27/52.
(Russ Reed Photo/Chini Collection)

Down the backstretch, heading for the "high" bank are Tony Sample (22), Johnny Soares (2), and Bud Rose (3). This was a WRA 250-lap race at Oakland on 6/26/49. Rose, a big car driver, had lots of experience on this track in the big cars.
(Russ Reed Photo/Chini Collection)

Walt James (15) and Jim Heath (1) tangle on the backstretch before a huge crowd at Oakland during a 250-lap race on 6/26/49. Both were injured and taken to a local hospital, checked out, and released.
(Russ Reed Photo/Chini Collection)

ROADSTER RACING AT OAKLAND

(Dana Photo by Rick/Jim Lamport Collection)

Roadster Racing at Oakland

Roadsters of the thirties, mostly factory roadster models with the fenders removed and their motors souped up, were being raced on oval tracks in northern California in an almost "amateur" fashion. There were few legitimate sanctions and even fewer monetary payoffs for winning. The biggest step made to legitimize these roadsters came when the two primary roadster clubs of the greater San Francisco Bay Area came together and formed the Bay Cities Roadster Racing Association[1] in 1939. At that point track promoters seriously began to promote the roadster races as a recognized form of motor sports racing.

Track Roadsters

Roadster racing was introduced to the Oakland Stadium in September 1946, a few months after the track was built. These races were exhibitions only, and most of the cars were holdovers from the street-roadster era: mainly fender-less Model "A" bodied roadsters with hopped up Ford or Mercury V-8 engines. As an outgrowth of the pre-war modified street roadsters, popular during the 1930s, it seemed only natural that the Oakland Stadium would showcase these particular types of race cars. Promoters began to us the term "track roadsters" to promote the cars, in the hopes that fans would not confuse them with street roadsters.

NCRRA

By the spring of 1947, the Northern California Roadster Racing Association (NCRRA) was formed. Its organization consisted of some pre-war cars, but more importantly, it also had a number of newly constructed cars that were made up strictly for oval track racing. These cars were really "street hot rods," mostly powered by hopped-up Ford or Mercury V-8 engines. Another change was taking place with the form itself: Most pre-war roadsters utilized Ford Model "A" bodies. The preferred body choice for most post-war roadsters was either the 1923 or 1925 Ford Model "T" roadster, commonly referred to as the "T-bucket" body.

The post-war roadsters were more highly modified than the pre-war versions. The motors were set back farther in the frames for better weight distribution, and the bodies were merely shells of the original Model "Ts." Most cars were equipped with a form of center steering, as opposed to the left-hand offset steering of the pre-war cars. This change placed the driver directly in the middle of the car, thereby necessitating the fashioning of a box type cockpit with a bucket seat placed directly in the center of the car.

Many of the modifications being made to the roadsters were in an effort to lighten the cars. Heavy engine flywheels

---

[1] Bay Cities Roadster Racing Association later re-formed as Bay Cities Racing Association, a midget racing organization. Readers can refer to *BCRA, The First 50 Years* (Published in 1990 by Tom Motter)

were eliminated (thereby eliminating the self-starter on the cars), and as there was now no clutch, the cars had to be push-started. Final drive gear ratios were accomplished by changing ring and pinion gears in the rear-end[2] and using Lincoln-Zephyr gears in the transmission (which was altered to run in one gear only[3]).

In 1947 roadster racing had become a very popular affair at most local tracks. The Oakland Stadium offered roadster races very Friday night during the season, usually running from March through October. These races, sanctioned by the NCRRA, were well run, highly paid events, and the huge crowds loved the fast action on Oakland's quarter-mile pavement.

The roadsters first attempt at running on the full 5/8-mile track occurred on October 19, 1947. That event, billed as "The First Annual Pacific Coast 100 Lap Hot Rod Championship Race," brought out all of the NCRRA regulars, including George Pacheco, Ed Elisian, Gene Tessien, Sam Hawks, Bob Veith, and Bob Machin, plus a number of drivers from the Central California Racing Association, all looking for a share of the prize money being offered. Larry Terra won the 100-lap affair, witnessed by a reported 8000 fans. Following Terra across the finish line were Lemoine Frey and Bob Machin. Bob Sweikert set fast time of the day at 24.74 seconds, 2 ½ seconds slower than the world's mark for the track.

NCRRA's 1948 season did not include racing at the Oakland track, with one exception. In the late fall of '48, NCRRA did run another 100-lap race at Oakland. This time it was called the "Oakland Stadium 100 Lap Hot Rod Invitational." As in '47, it was also held on the full 5/8-mile track.

RRI

During the 1947 season the NCRRA paid out nearly $125,000 in prize money, giving the promoters of the other local Bay Area tracks reason to take notice. The 1948 season started with the formation of a new roadster association. It appears that a consortium of owners/managers of the San Jose, Belmont, Salinas, and Oakland tracks saw the opportunity to gain more control of the purse situation and formed RRI (Roadster Racing Incorporated). Drivers and owners wishing to run at any of those tracks had to join the RRI, or not run. Most of the top NCRRA drivers elected not to join RRI, but to stay and race at most of the San Joaquin Valley tracks such as the Stockton and Modesto 99 Speedways, Hughes Stadium and the Lazy J Speedway in Sacramento, and at the Contra Costa and Santa Rosa tracks in the Bay Area. Among those NCRRA drivers that went over to the RRI were Al Slinker, Bob Sweikert, Don Kolb, Johnny Keys, and Elmer George.

The RRI race held at Oakland on July 25, 1948 occasioned a spectacular crash. The next day, the *Oakland Post Enquirer* announced "4 Cars Crash in Oakland Stadium Race." The article continued, "Scheduled for 40 laps, yesterday's Racing Roadsters Inc. Assoc. program before a crowd of 7,500 fans was stopped at 30 laps because of a 4 car crash. Troy Ruttman, leading at the time, was declared the winner of the event. Jim Davies, involved in the accident was awarded 2nd, Bud Kelleher, third." Local photographer Eric Rickman, shooting for Dana Photo, captured

---

[2] By this time, a number of the roadsters were using quick-change gear boxes and a few even had quick-change rear-ends.

[3] Cars having regular transmissions usually ran second gear only on the quarter mile tracks.

the complete action in a spectacular fifteen-shot sequence that appears in Don Radbruch's book, *Roaring Roadsters*[4].

Disaster!

In the summer of 1949, hardtop racing was introduced to the racing fans at the Oakland Stadium (as well as at most of the other tracks in the greater Bay Area). Immediately, the fan base at the roadster races began to suffer. The roadster racing was exciting, but the show put on by the hardtops was much more action-packed, with their many crashes and rollovers. By the end of the '49 season the roadster associations knew that they were in trouble! The number of roadster races held during the next few years began to dwindle noticeably. In the words of popular roadster driver Bob Machin[5], "It was a disaster! Hardtop racing ruined the roadsters."

Dissension Within the Ranks

By 1953, the inter-association strife that had crippled so many other racing associations had finally done the same thing to track roadster racing. The quarreling about purses and the dissension between car owners, drivers, and tracks concerning all aspects of the racing game had an effect on race fans. Fewer cars showing up at tracks meant fewer fans in the grandstands. One more association would try to present roadster racing to the Oakland Stadium fans.

Bob Barkhimer, a former BCRA business manager and their 1945 driving champion, had finally decided that promoting races[6] instead of driving race cars was a safer and more lucrative way to make living. "Barkie" had been promoting races in the greater Bay Area for several years, and in 1953 decided to form an association for race cars in addition to the Cal Stock hardtops that he had under his control.

WCRA

The West Coast Racing Association was formed expressly to bring together the cars and drivers from various racing groups: roadsters, stock cars, sports cars and sprint cars. Each of these groups[7] seemed to have problems in putting on a competitive show for the fans. WCRA's first sanctioned race, held on March 8, 1953, was also the season's opener[8]. Ed Lockhart of Venice, California won the 40-lap event before a crowd of 5200 race fans[9]. Lemoine Frey placed 2nd, Sam Hawks 3rd, Jerry Hill 4th, and Don Radbruch 5th.

"WCRA ROADSTERS TO ROAR AGAIN AT OAKLAND ON SUNDAY, MAY 31, 1953" proclaimed the *Oakland Tribune* sports section. It went on to say that "the roaring hot

---

[4] Readers who wish to read a more complete history of roadster racing in this country are advised to refer to Don Radbruch's great work on the subject, *Roaring Roadsters*, published in 1994. Don's book is considered the definitive work on roadsters. He can be contacted at 450 Road 39G, Sagle, ID 83860.

[5] Besides being a top roadster pilot in the N.C.R.R.A., Machin was its President in 1947.

[6] In 1949 Barkhimer formed the California Stock Car Racing Association in northern California. His first promotion, a hardtop race at San Jose Speedway had six cars participating. Ultimately Barkhimer had some 20-22 racetracks in California and southern Oregon under his control. C.S.C.R.A. was to become the third largest racing association in the country, behind U.S.A.C. and N.A.S.C.A.R.

[7] C.S.R.A.'s hardtops (under Barkie's control) and B.C.R.A.'s midgets were the only successful weekly race sanctioning bodies operating in northern California at the time with the possible exception of the A.R.A. sprint cars.

[8] This race was run on the full 5/8-mile but below the white line, not up against the outside wall.

[9] The *Oakland Tribune* reported this as being "the largest crowd that had been seen in years".

rods return to the Oakland Speedway tomorrow for the second program of the West Coast Racing Association's double speedway show on the 5/8-mile asphalt track."

The first race of the double-header was a 100-mile big car event held on Saturday, May 30th, and won by Jack Flaherty of San Francisco, followed by Eli Vukovich,[10] Bob Kelleher, and Jim Bloberger in that order.

The second race of the Memorial Day weekend, a 20-lap roadster race held on Sunday, May 31st, was also run on the full 5/8-mile track. George Mahalis won the 20-lap feature. Placing second was Bob Schellinger, with Bob Machin taking third place. Bob Veith, who won the trophy dash, had been leading the feature race through lap 16, when he was forced out because of mechanical problems. Mahalis took over on lap 17, and was never headed. Don Radbruch, who in pre-race publicity had been favored to cop the checkered flag, didn't compete for some unknown reason[11].

Last Roadster Race at Oakland

The Fourth of July weekend, historically, has been a big auto-racing weekend in this country. Northern California, in 1953, was no exception.

Oakland's WCRA had scheduled a racing double-header for July 4th, with a combination of roadster and big car racing on the full 5/8-mile track[12]. With a short field of sprint cars available, the promoters decided to run the sprint car main event with only 15 laps. Local driver Clyde Palmer won the 15-lap main event.

The roadster race was advertised at 20 laps. Here again there was a shortage of cars. Many of the roadsters had been changed over to their sprint car configuration and were running at Calistoga and Oroville that weekend. Lemoine Frey, one of the outstanding local roadster regulars, copped the 20-lap feature, with Bob Machin taking second place. Machin also won the roadster trophy dash.

It's interesting to note that a display ad in the *Tribune* (7/4/53) listed admission prices as follows: adults, $1.80, children, 50 cents!

Training Ground for Many

It must be remembered that some of the finest open wheel drivers of the 1950s had their roots buried deep in the banks of Oakland's high-banked 5/8-mile track. Ed Elisian and Bob Veith, both Oakland residents, started their racing careers in the roadster ranks at the Oakland Stadium. Bob Sweikert[13], a Hayward resident, started his racing career in the roadsters at Oakland. Elmer George (father of Tony George, currently president of the Indianapolis Motor Speedway) a resident of Salinas, California, honed his driving skills in a roadster at Oakland. Another prominent driver of the '50s, Troy Ruttman[14], got plenty of seat time in Oakland roadster racing.

---

[10] While Eli, younger brother of Bill Vukovich, was taking a second place at Oakland, Bill had just won the '53 Indianapolis 500 race.

[11] Radbruch, in recalling those hectic racing days of 1953, thinks this was about the time he decided to "retire" from the dangers of Big Car and Roadster competition.

[12] Most of the sprint car owners and drivers would be appearing at Napa County Fair races held at Calistoga on Friday night, July 3rd and Sunday night, July 5th. They also ran a sprint car program at Oroville Speedway on Saturday afternoon, July 4th which turned out to be a bust. Despite a goodly amount of advertising, most Sacramento Valley race fans were aware that the track at Oroville would be a hot (!), dusty affair with little or no shade available for the spectators. They stayed away in droves.

[13] Winner of the 1955 Indianapolis 500.

[14] Winner of the 1952 Indianapolis 500.

All of these men later went on to race with AAA's sprint car division in the Midwest. While many of their contemporaries were intimidated by the so-called "high banks" of Winchester, Salem, and Dayton Speedways, these Oakland "graduates" were quite comfortable running those tracks. After all, Oakland's banks were nearly twice as steep as any of the Indiana/Ohio tracks. The speeds at Oakland were also greater.

Roadsters Become Sprint Cars

In the end, the demise of the Oakland Stadium was generally coincidental with the end of roadster racing. By 1953 most of the roadster owners had realized that sprint car racing was paying bigger purses.

It was a relatively simple matter to replace the roadster body with a sprint car body and go sprint car racing. The chassis and running gear were generally the same for both types of cars and the change-over could easily be accomplished in a few hours.

By 1954 there were few, if any, roadster races being run in northern California, and there were none held at Oakland that last year. 1954 was also the end of all racing at the Oakland Stadium.

Urban sprawl, along with rising land values, coupled with poor crowds and even poorer racing finally brought an end to the life of the track. It was soon to be torn down and replaced by a huge shopping center; a common scenario repeated throughout many communities in this country.

Only in the last half of this past decade have developers finally become interested in building a number of huge racing complexes. These "new" racing facilities have been strategically placed in mega-populated communities and are geared to "special racing events only" as presented by NASCAR, CART, and IRL.

J. D. Bennett (a.k.a. Jim Lamport), runs up high on the 62° high bank at Oakland. This was a 1949, 50-lap feature. J.D. placed 4th. Since Jim was only 18 years old he used his friend's (J. D. Bennett) I.D. to prove he was old enough to go racing.
(Dana Photo by Rick/Jim Lamport Collection)

Bob Veith started his racing career in the roadsters here at Oakland Stadium. Veith raced midgets, champ cars, and drove in the Indy 500 eleven times from '56-'69.
(Lafayette Photo/Chini Collection)

This 1946 ad is from the Oakland Stadium's first "Memorial Program." The All-American Soap Box Derby was held at the stadium during 1946-47-48.
(Motter Collection)

On the pole, Jim Alger (121), Herb Hill (outside, 1st row), Al Slinker (inside, 2nd row), and Ed Elisian (outside, 2nd) make this main event start at Oakland. Dotted white line on track is to keep the cars off of the high wall during this race. Races on the high wall tended to be one big "parade lap" with little or no passing.
(Russ Reed Photo/Chini Collection)

Elmer George in Bob Shirley's roadster up on the high-bank at Oakland. Elmer went on to race sprint, champ cars, and ran in three Indy 500s during the '50s. Elmer also is the father of Tony George, President of the IMS and the IRL.
(Rod Eschenburg Collection)

The All American Soap Box Derby

One of Charlie Curryer's dreams for the Oakland Stadium was that of having the facility used for sporting events other than auto racing. When Chevrolet Motor Car Division of General Motors (the originator and national sponsor of the event) announced the All American Soap Box Derby would be resumed after the war, Curryer was quick to offer the stadium as the site for the 1946 event. He donated the funds to build the special coasting ramp, as well as provided at no charge the staff and officials used during the event.

The Oakland *Post-Enquirer* (the local sponsor) began a month-long campaign promoting the first post-war event, open to boys aged eleven to fifteen, to be held on Saturday, July 27, 1946 at the newly built Oakland Stadium. The derbies were also held at the stadium (thanks to Curryer) in 1947 and '48.

Don Scott, an Oakland Hills resident of fifteen, realized that this would be his last year of eligibility for the event and urged his brother Dick to join with him in building a Soap Box Derby racer. Dick, two years younger than Don, deciding that he'd rather have his own racer to enter in the July '48 event, set about building his own car.

Don, an avid auto racing fan, had been to the Oakland Stadium on many occasions with his parents and was smitten with the thought of someday being able to drive a race car on the exciting Oakland 5/8-mile track. Here, at last, was the opportunity for Don to finally get out on the track, even if it wasn't in a real race car.

Both boys immediately began construction on their respective cars. Derby rules absolutely required that the cars be completely built by the youngsters themselves, with no help from adults. They also required that no more than $10.00 be spent on the project (with the exception of the cost of the "Official Soap Box Derby Wheels"). These were purchased, and soon the Scott boys were ready to go racing.

Once at the track, both boys came face to face with the newly constructed, very high coasting ramp. The grade looked a lot steeper than either boy had imagined, and it was with some trepidation that they finally got lined up in their heat races.

With a crowd of nearly 10,000 spectators looking on, younger brother Dick was soon at the top of the ramp ready for the headlong dash to the bottom. The barrier was released and away he went! Down the ramp, onto the pavement of the actual track, heading for the finish line 600 feet away. The winner was none other than Dick Scott in his number 42 racer. Meanwhile, older brother Don was at the bottom of the ramp, watching his little brother, taking notes on just how he might be

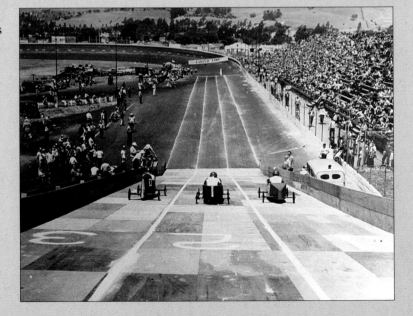

Three closely matched racers head for the finish line. Dick Scott, center lane, wins his heat while younger brother, Don (bottom of ramp) urges him on.
(Don Scott Collection)

Don Scott (center) takes second in his heat.
(Don Scott Collection)

able to better his position when his heat race came up.

While it was apparent to both boys that a number of the cars that showed up that day weren't entirely built by the participants themselves (as the rules called for), there was still hope that Don could also place his racer in the winner's circle. Don's turn was next, sitting in his own Derby racer at the Oakland Stadium, waiting for the chance to earn his spot in racing stardom. The barricade was released! Away he went, racing towards the finish line and the run-out area just past the finish line that led to that famous, high-banked, turn two of Oakland's high wall.

Unfortunately, Don wasn't the winner of his heat race, and was eliminated from any further events. It was to be the end of his racing career.

Dick Scott (with parents) receives trophy.
(Don Scott Collection)

Dick Scott, winner, flashes across finish line!
(Don Scott Collection)

Popular roadster driver Jumpin' Joe Valenti is surrounded by pit crew and fans after a race at Oakland.
(Russ Reed Photo/Chini Collection)

Gene Tessien (L) and Ed Elisian (R) are having a good time during the pre-race publicity photos for the 8/51 roadster race at Oakland. Unfortunately, the two pretty ladies are unidentified.
(Russ Reed Photo/Randy Reed Collection)

Larry Terra in the Tony Cancilla roadster at Oakland. "Hisso" was a reference to the Hisso motor that was half of a V-8 aircraft engine used in some "big cars."
(Dana Photo by Rick/Chini Collection)

Sam Hawks in the Herk Viglienzone "Stockton Spitfire" roadster at Oakland. Herk's Spitfire was Chrysler 6-cylinder powered, rather than the much more common Ford V-8 power plant.
(Randy Viglienzone Collection)

One of the pioneers in Bay Area roadster racing was Dick Hubbard (wearing glasses). Hubbard Auto Parts was a big sponsor of racing at Oakland. This is his first roadster, built in 1946. Sitting in the car is Bob Marcoe.
(Rushing/Elisian Collection)

Parade lap on the 5/8-mile at Oakland. Russ Reed took great photos at Oakland; too bad there's no driver identification. *(Russ Reed Photo/Chini Collection)*

Elmer George in the Bob Shirley Mercury at Oakland in 1950.
(Don Radbruch Collection)

Sam Hawks in the Pestana-George roadster built by Jack Hagemann in 1948. The car had a tubular frame, quite unusual for the period.
(Motter Collection)

Gene Tessien gets introduced before an event at Oakland.
(Rushing/Elisian Collection)

Earl Motter in one of only two appearances in a track roadster. Here he's in Don Kolb's #69 at Oakland for a 40-lapper on March 8, 1953. Motter was better known for his ability in midgets and champ cars.
(Russ Reed Photo/Chini Collection)

The car was owned by Bob Rushing and being driven by George Danburg at Oakland in 1948.
(Dana Photo by Rick/Chini Collection)

Here's another one of those spectacular Russ Reed photos taken at the Oakland Stadium. At least there was plenty of room to maneuver on Oakland's high-banks. Gino Birgnardello (50), Cliff Peters (77), Elmer George (86), and Bob Shellenger (5) are among the group in action during this 1951 race.
(Russ Reed Photo/Chini Collection)

Chet Richards was in the McFadden Ford Six at this 1950 RRI race at Oakland.
(Don Radbruch Collection)

Right outside of the Oakland Stadium, on East 14th Street, were two 40-foot long billboards owned by the Stadium. This one advertised the "Roaring Roadsters."
(Don Radbruch Collection)

Ben Hubbard giving Bob Machin a little "fatherly" advice at Oakland in 1947. Machin was one of the stars of roadster racing that went on to midgets with BCRA and USAC.
(Russ Reed Photo/Chini Collection)

This Ad appeared in the 1947 Oakland Stadium programs announcing the weekly Roadster Races. These races were run on the 1/4-mile track.
(Motter Collection)

Eighteen-year-old Jim Lamport drove under the name of J.D. Bennett. Here he is in 1950, ready to run a 50-lap roadster race at the Oakland Stadium. In the "old days" you had to be 21 to drive a race car.
(Dana Photo by Rick/Jim Lamport Collection)

Roadsters line up at Oakland's 5/8-mile for an RRI race on the high-banked track. Jim Alger (121), Herb Hill (9), Al Slinker (inside, 2nd row), and Ed Elisian (outside, 2nd row).
(Russ Reed Photo/Chini Collection)

Mel Alexander at Oakland in a 1948 NCRRA race. In the background is the number one turn, only 35° banking. Looks like someone dumped water or oil on the track.
(Motter Collection)

Ed Elisian in the Ben Sanders/George Rowell roadster at Oakland in 1948.
(Don Radbruch Collection)

George Pacheco, 1947 NCRRA champion.
(Russ Reed Photo/Chini Collection)

HARDTOP RACING AT OAKLAND

Russ Reed Photo/Chini Collection

Hardtop Racing at Oakland

"HARD TOP RACES, WATCH FOR OPENING DATE, Oakland Stadium, every Tuesday Night" read an ad appearing in a roadster race program in mid-1949.

The "how" and "why" of hardtop auto racing, as introduced to Bay Area race fans, came about due to a very interesting set of circumstances.

By 1949 people involved in midget racing realized the crowds of the previous three seasons just weren't there. Lots of theories were tossed about. Television, a new form of entertainment, was keeping families home at night instead of coming out to the race tracks as they had during 1946, '47, and '48. Another theory, not nearly as popular but probably much more telling, went that after three years of seven-nights-a-week midget racing, crowds were tiring of looking at the same old thing.

The near-assembly line produced Kurtis Kraft midgets in 1946 had, by 1949, finally caught up with the fans. Most midgets on the track were all very nearly look-alikes except for the paint job and the number painted on the tail.

The fans were bored.

Enter (or, re-enter) one Robert Barkhimer. "Barkie" was not new to the racing scene. A chance visit to a midget race at the Emeryville Speedway in 1937 started him on the path to a career in auto racing that lasted many, many years.

He raced midgets in the years before World War II, when all midgets were the creation of individuals who had different ideas about what this "new" development in auto racing should be about. After the war ended Barkhimer took up where he had left off in 1941, but with a greater vengeance and a better race car. Barkie, in the Abdo Allen Drake midget, won BCRA's abbreviated 1945 season! In 1948 he took over the business management of Bay Cities Racing Association, but not for long, as Barkie wanted to do some things that the midget association just didn't understand.

Barkhimer Predicts the Future

He was predicting the end of the popular, seven-night-a-week racing that was going on at the time. He also said that hardtops (or modified stock car bodied cars) were going to be the rage of the future. Articles in the *Illustrated Speedway News*[1] had convinced Barkie that hardtop racing, with its intense, crowd-pleasing antics, would be the racing entertainment of the future. He was right; within a few short years the crowds began filling the grandstands again!

Barkhimer proposed to the BCRA board of directors that they form a hardtop division to take up the slack that the midgets were losing. The notion wasn't popular with the board members and soon Barkie, along with probably the only other believer

---

[1] *Illustrated Speedway News* and its successor, *National Speed Sport News* chronicled all automobile racing news in the country. It was here that "Barkie" first noticed the popularity of hardtop racing in other parts of the country.

(Jerry Piper), was out the door. Barkie then made a proposal to Freddie Agabashian and Jerry Piper (two of northern California's most popular midget drivers) to become equal partners in a new association. Aggie, although interested, dropped out before the formation took place, but Piper stayed[2].

Barkie, who already was managing the San Jose Speedway, went ahead and organized his own California Stock Car Racing Association and made the San Jose track his headquarters. The first race held by CSCRA was at San Jose on August 6, 1949. The program consisted of twelve cars (which included Jerry Piper at the wheel of one of them) with 400 fans in the grandstand. Within two years, Barkie's CSCRA boasted more than 1000 members racing more than 500 hardtops on fourteen different tracks weekly in central and northern California.

BCRA Forms "Hardtop Division"

Apparently, Barkie's discussion of a hardtop division had not fallen on completely deaf ears. By August 1949, Bay Cities Racing Association had inaugurated its own, brand-new "hardtop" division. The first race was held at the Oakland Stadium. Business Manager Jack London, realizing that his midget association wasn't drawing the crowds the track promoters wanted, began making deals with the various tracks to hold "combination" races, offering both midgets and the new hardtops. Tuesday nights at the Oakland Stadium became known as "hardtop night," and lasted several years. Ultimately it became so popular that, by 1950, a local television station began broadcasting a live half-hour remote from the track on Tuesday nights, starting at 9:00 p.m.[3].

BCRA's first hardtop race on August 9, 1949 at Oakland included the midget division. Johnny Soares was the fast qualifier of the night at 19.65 seconds[4]. Soares, starting last in the trophy dash, won the four-lap event, beating out Johnny Smith, Eddie Bennett, and Cliff Roberts. The first three heat winners were Everett Evans, Bud Williamson, and Ted Hansen. During the third heat, former roadster driver Bob Rushing caused a yellow flag when he spun out, scattering the field. The fourth heat was a dilly, cars being pushed and shoved all over the track. Marvin Burke locked a front bumper with the rear bumper of another car and was dragged sideways down the length of the front straightaway before the brackets gave way and released him. Eddie Bennet slipped by in the excitement to win, coming up from sixth spot, ahead of Smith, Roberts, and Soares in the very fast time of 2:49.90 seconds. It was at this point (after the heat races) that the fog rolled in and the rest of the program had to be cancelled.

---

[2] Jerry Piper, a popular midget driver, was suspended by B.C.R.A. and his accumulated 1949 points were taken away. At the time, Piper was leading the B.C.R.A. points chase. B.C.R.A. felt that his involvement with Barkhimer's plan to start a modified stock car racing association was a conflict of interest with the midget association.

[3] Ironically, it was television that had been one of the contributing factors leading to the declining crowds at the race tracks in 1949. Although the "live" TV coverage didn't last more than several months it is now seen as a trend-setting idea that today accounts for the huge following of stock car racing in this country.

[4] These races were all run on the smaller quarter mile track (inside the 5/8-mile).

[5] Many of the earliest hardtop pilots came from the ranks of B.C.R.A.'s midget racing division. Drivers such as Mike McGreevy, Dickie Reese, Johnny Soares and even George Bignotti, B.C.R.A.'s noted midget championship car owner, were frequently in the line-up at B.C.R.A.'s hardtop races.

The first complete hardtop race at Oakland was run the next week (August 16, 1949). It also was a combo program with the midgets, and midget pilot Ed Normi[5] won the 50-lap main event. The highlight of the feature was the feud between Johnny Soares and Harry Schilling. Soares spun Shilling off the track while trying to get by, but Shilling came back with "blood in his eyes" and took out after Soares' little '36 Ford coupe. Shilling's big, heavy 1949 Mercury wasn't able to catch him.

The First Years

The first season for the BCRA hardtops at Oakland (1949) was a short one. Johnny Soares, driving the Bob Feehan Ford coupe, was crowned the Hardtop Champion for the '49 season[6], a feat that he repeated in 1950. Cliff Roberts won the championship in 1951, while Keith Willis captured the title in 1952.

BCRA wasn't the only association to sanction hardtop racing at the Oakland Stadium. By 1950 Barkhimer and Billy Hunefeld[7] had leased the Oakland track and began a series of promotions under the banner of a new group called the West Coast Racing Association (WCRA). Basically, this association combined both the BCRA and CSCRA groups, in an effort to bring about a uniting of the various sanctioning bodies in the greater Bay Area. The WCRA group sanctioned several notable races at Oakland between 1950 and 1953. On July 16, 1950 a major stock car race sanctioned by BCRA, held on the 5/8-mile track, featured many of the drivers from the two previously mentioned associations. On May 4, 1952, WCRA hosted a hardtop "championship race" on the full 5/8-mile track that brought cars and drivers from all over northern and central California. Local *Oakland Tribune* photographer, Russ Reed, an avid race fan and hardtop owner himself, was on assignment that day covering the action for the *Tribune*. One of his photographs was picked by *Life* magazine as Sports Photo of the Year, an award that was presented him on the Ed Sullivan Show later that fall.

On August 5, 1952 Johnny Soares once again showed his adaptability at driving a variety of race cars. Soares had entered the hardtop program with the intention of making an assault on the (hardtop) one-lap track record, which stood at 18.08 seconds[8]. The previous week Soares had won a 300-lap stock car race at Oakland.

One month later, on September 14, 1952, Soares, driving a 1950 Oldsmobile, won a 350-lap late model stock car race at the same track. This race was sanctioned by CSCRA and BCRA, but listed in the program as a WCRA race.

Bill Maher

Bill Maher, one of the graduates of the Massa/Bennett Midget Racing School[9], had realized that the hardtop racing was a much less expensive way to break into the local racing scene. As one of the earliest BCRA members to join the hardtop division, Bill's rise to the top of the point standings came quickly. Maher finished fifth in the '50 season, fourth in '51, and second

---

[6] Soares, a competitor in the pre-war modified street roadsters, moved over to the midgets during the 1945 racing season. He did well in the midgets, placing 15th in '45, 5th in '46, 6th in '47, 5th in '48 and 10th in 1949.

[7] Bill Hunefeld a promoter from the San Joaquin Valley, promoted races, both before and after WWII, at tracks such as Lodi's Grape Bowl, Stockton's Baxter Stadium and at Sacramento's Hughes Stadium.

[8] Soares had set the initial record at the track three years earlier at 19.65 seconds.

[9] In 1948 midget car owner Jimmy Massa and Eddie Bennett formed a driving school dedicated to teaching novice drivers the fine art of race car driving. The Oakland Stadium was the track used as their base of operations.

in '52. Now driving the Jack Davis Hudson, he missed a good portion of the 1953 season due to a cracked pelvis, an injury suffered at a Vallejo Speedway incident early in the year. As the season drew to a close, Bill was in a tight race for the championship with Keith Willis who was driving the Alameda Auto Wreckers' car. So important was the Oakland track to the success of the hardtop programs that it would be there that the 1953 season championship would be decided for Bill.

The 1953 Hardtop Season

An incident at Oakland involving Maher's good friend Cliff Roberts, ultimately led to the '53 championship for Bill. Maher was trailing Keith Willis by several points, when one night late in the season Jack Davis, Bill's car owner, told him that he wouldn't be able to bring the car to Oakland because repairs hadn't been completed in time.

Roberts, driving an underpowered Dodge, had managed to win four straight main events at Oakland and was shooting for his fifth in a row. When Cliff asked Bill where the Hudson was that night, Bill's reply was that Davis couldn't make it with the car. Cliff immediately said, "I'm glad. I don't feel too hot—how about driving the Dodge?" Bill Maher was pretty sure that there was nothing wrong with his friend, and that he just wanted to see Bill stay in the tight points chase with Willis. Bill told him that he didn't want to deny his friend the opportunity to win five in a row, and declined the offer to drive his car. But Cliff was adamant and said that if Bill didn't drive it he'd have to find someone else to do it.

Years later, Maher admitted that he had always felt guilty about accepting Cliff's ride that night. As it happened, Bill won that night's feature in his friend's car, and the forty or so points edge it gave him over Keith Willis was enough to win the championship. When the season ended, Maher had won the championship by a mere twelve points[10] over Willis. Maher always insisted that Cliff had handed him the championship that night by insisting that he drive his car.

Hardtop racing, under the BCRA and WCRA banners, would continue at Oakland through 1952. By 1953 Barkhimer had given up the leases on the Oakland Stadium, and was concentrating on his ever-expanding Cal Stock Association. In 1954 he associated his tracks and hardtop group with NASCAR[11], beginning a long-time business arrangement that was financially profitable for both Barkie and Bill France of NASCAR.

Hardtops or Jalopies?

After Barkie pulled out of the management of the Oakland Stadium in '52, it was taken over by Harry Schilling and "Mack" McGrete. By 1954, the last year of operations at the track, most of the hardtop races run at the track were actually jalopy races. Schilling and McGrete promoted these races, with the help of Business Manager Jack Smith, under the name of the Oakland Racing Association. ORA was strictly an "in-house" association, meant to sanction races at the Oakland track only.

These races were held on a weekly basis with a few "special events" thrown in during the 1954 racing season. The *Tribune* was still referring to them as hardtop races, while the

---

[10] During the years that the hardtops were running it wasn't unusual to see the crowned champion with a point total of over 3000 points.
[11] The National Association of Stock Car Auto Racing had been primarily a regional (southeastern U.S.) racing organization. Its president, Bill France, was desirous of bring the West Coast into his fold in order to satisfy national sponsorship. By bringing Barkhimer and his tracks into the NASCAR family, France was able to show sponsors that he truly was a "National" racing organization, with races run "coast-to-coast."

programs sold at the track referred to them as "jalopy races." Most of the entrants were not from any of the existing hardtop associations (BCRA and CSCRA,) but were a new group of owners and drivers looking to make a name for themselves in the local racing circles.

By 1954 the track's two high-banked turns had been filled in with dirt, and the track circumference was cut back from the original 5/8-mile to a 1/2-mile combination dirt/pavement track. Most of the weekly races held on the original 1/4-mile surface were usually limited to 25-lap main events. There were hardtop races held on Memorial Day weekend (Monday, May 31, 1954), but the last big event for the hardtops at Oakland was held on July 4th, 1954, and was billed as "A Pacific Coast Stock Hard Top Championship." It was held on the new 1/2-mile track, but by that time the promoters were calling the facility the "Oakland Speedway"[13]. Dick Carter (not to be confused with roadster driver Dave Carter) won the 30-lap race.

Jalopy Races Produce a "Star"

One of northern California's most promising young race drivers, Dick Atkins, came from the ranks of the Oakland Racing Association's jalopies. The eighteen-year-old youngster, from nearby Hayward, won his first main event at one of the jalopy races held at Oakland in 1954.

Atkins learned his craft quickly. In 1958 he began racing midgets with Bay Cities Racing Association, and by 1962 placed within the top ten finishers for the season. In 1964, driving for Sim Clark, he took the BCRA driving title, a feat he repeated in 1965. In 1966 he won BCRA's indoor midget crown.

It looked as if Atkins was headed for super-star status when promoter-car owner J.C. Agajanian entered him in the 1966 Indy 500. There he qualified as first alternate starter, and in October he won the 100-mile champ car race in Sacramento. Unfortunately, two weeks later he was fatally injured in a sprint car race at Ascot Park in southern California.

It's All Over

As it happened, the 1954 racing season was to be the last at the Oakland Stadium. The hardtops were the last programs to be run on the track. The roadsters went away, and in most cases those that survived were converted to sprint car bodies. Midgets, last seen at Oakland in 1953, were to become far less popular than they had been earlier. Late model stock cars made only a few more appearances in northern California, mainly at Bay Meadows in '55 & '56 and at the Vallejo 5/8-mile track. The sprint cars lost popularity with the fans and didn't make a resurgence until after 1960, when the Northern Auto Racing Club took over the reins from Charlie Curryer's original ARA.

Only the hardtops survived. Every race track in northern and central California was running a weekly hardtop program of some sort long after the Oakland Stadium was torn down in 1955. Barkie had been right! The hardtops were the wave of the future for racing in the Bay Area as well as the rest of the country.

---

[12] Obviously the management of the track couldn't decide which name they wanted the track to be known by. "Oakland Stadium" was the name given the track when first built by Charlie Curryer in 1946. "Oakland Speedway" was the name of the "Stadium's" predecessor, the one-mile track of pre-war fame built in 1931.

Chuck Mount (94X), Gene Costa (273), Bob Wilhelm (35), Bud Olson (179), Jack Beaver (90), and Tom Watkins (142) are the identifiable drivers in this shot taken at Oakland on 5/4/52.
(Russ Reed Photo/Silva-Blado Collection)

Clyde Palmer (141x) has the pole position at the start of this event at Oakland on 5/4/52. On the outside of Palmer is Tommy Ornellas (128). Behind Palmer is Leo Barlest (178).
(Russ Reed Photo/Motter Collection)

Gene Costa (273) climbs out of his car, helmet off, through for the moment. Bud Olson (179) and Jack Beaver (90) have parked their cars also. George Hopkins (108) goes by high up on the bank. This race was run on the full 5/8-mile course at Oakland on 5/4/52.
(Russ Reed Photo/Silva-Blado Collection)

Al Pombo, (circle 3), starts on the pole with Lee Humphers (5) on the outside in this event at Oakland. CSCRA and BCRA co-sanctioned this 50-lap event and it drew a number of cars from the San Joaquin Valley that didn't normally run at the Oakland Stadium.
(Dennis Arnold Photo/Don Bishop Collection)

Oakland Tribune photographer Russ Reed's own caption on this photo reads "Start & finish of race on lap no. 1 at Oakland 5/8-mile." This photo was awarded "Picture of the Week" by *Life* magazine for the week of 5/4/52. Russ was presented the award on the Ed Sullivan TV show. This was a 50-lap race on the full 5/8-mile track that drew over 120 entries from all of northern and central California. Rod Zanoline of Healdsburg, California won it.
(Russ Reed Photo/Motter Collection)

Thrill Circus Comes to Oakland!

(Reprinted from an Oakland Stadium Official Program, June 10, 1951)

The show that has thrilled fans from coast to coast comes to the Oakland Stadium Monday night, June 11th for one performance only. Billed as the 1951 International Championship open stunt contest and combined Joie Chitwood Auto Daredevils thrill circus.

In all there will be 28 exciting events, including seeing four cars completely demolished in the roll-over contest; broadjumping new 1951 Ford Sedans more than 100 feet into the air and over three other cars racing underneath; crashing sedans into a solid wall of ice; crashing two sedans head-on into each other at better than 60 miles-per-hour; stepping from the rear of speeding cars into pools of flaming gasoline; two-wheel precision driving and stock car steeplechase.

Broadjumping motorcycles for distance and through blazing hoops; crashing through blazing plank walls and headlined by Lucky Walters, "the human bomb," who will blow himself up in a casket with 20 sticks of dynamite.

Team entries include Chitwood Auto Daredevils, Detroit, Michigan, Angel Lopez y su Diablos Del Timon, Mexico City; Harry Woolman's Hollywood Stuntmen and Bill Ward's Canadian Aces.

Gates of the Oakland Stadium will be opened at 6:30 p.m. with the first event scheduled to start at approximately 8:30. Remember the date, tomorrow night, Monday, June 11th.

Joie Chitwood introduced "Auto Daredevil Show" to crowd at Oakland Stadium, October, 1949.
(Don Scott Photo/Collection)

Stunt man, Tommy "Lucky Les" Lester, heads for wall of fire at Stunt Show performed at intermission during a hardtop race at Oakland Stadium on June 12, 1954. Ken Urton pilots the car towards wall.
(Ken Urton Collection)

Bob Rushing (7), pictured in his own car, was at the first BCRA hardtop race at Oakland in 1949. Rushing also drove track roadsters at Oakland.
(Rushing-Elisian Collection)

Hugh Purdy (pictured with trophy and "Miss Centennial") won the trophy dash at the 50-lap "Oakland Centennial Hardtop Championship" race held on 5/4/52. Following Purdy in the dash were Rod Zanolini, Lee Humphers, Johnny Smith, and Mel West.
(Russ Reed Photo/Chini Collection)

Dickie Reese (69) was a top midget chauffer and took only an occasional ride in a hardtop. Here he is at Oakland Stadium in 1951.
(Dickie Reese Collection)

More action during the 50-lap "Oakland Centennial" hardtop race on 5/4/52. Bill Williams (411) and Johnny Keyes (2x) out of shape in the middle of the pack. Others in the field are Cliff Roberts (1), Keith Willis (2), Lamar Barron (30), Joe Guisti (82), Bob Simpson (38), Les Stern (167), Marvin Panch (19), and Joe Valenti (57x).
(Russ Reed Photo/Motter Collection)

BCRA hardtops at Oakland, 7/8/50. Johnny Smith (12) leads George Bignotti (4), Frank Santos (13), and Johnny Soares (1) through turn two. Soares was BCRA's 1950 hardtop champion. George Bignotti has "more wins" as chief mechanic at the Indianapolis Motor Speedway than any man in its history.
(Russ Reed Photo/Chini Collection)

The 50-lap main event started the forty fastest qualifiers for the "Oakland Centennial Hardtop Championships" held on 5/4/52 at the Oakland Stadium. This shot shows half of the entire field! BCRA's 1951 hardtop champion, Cliff Roberts (1), started mid-field.
(Russ Reed Photo/Motter Collection)

This was one of the consolation heats held on 5/4/52. Jerry Wright (65) spins off the high wall and is tagged by Leo Barlest (178). Others identified are Chuck Ford (97), Bud Olson (179), and Tommy Ornellas (128). Chuck Ford went on to win the heat race.
(Russ Reed Photo/Motter Collection)

No, it's not a wrecking yard! This is the infield and part of the over 120 entries in the "Oakland Centennial Hardtop Championships" race held at the Oakland Stadium on 5/4/52. Team cars of Al Pombo (circle 3) and Archie Tucker (circle 23) came up from Fresno for the event. *(Dennis Arnold Photo/Don Bishop Collection)*

This ad appeared in the *Oakland Tribune* in 1949. It announces the very first BCRA hardtop races run at the Oakland Stadium. All of the drivers listed in the ad were BCRA midget drivers… they didn't yet have a listing of hardtop drivers.
(Motter Collection)

BCRA hardtop race at Oakland on 7/8/50. That's Bill Maher (58) bringing up the rear. Bill was BCRA champion in '53-'54.
(Russ Reed Photo/Chini Collection)

Oakland Tribune photographer Russ Reed owned this hardtop. Painted on the door is the question, "Wanna buy a picture?" Ed Normi is the driver.
(Russ Reed Photo/Randy Reed Collection)

How steep were the 62-degree banks at Oakland? Gordy Sutherland shows you!
(Gordy Sutherland Collection)

IN CONCLUSION

Russ Reed Photo/Chini Collection

In Conclusion

As early as 1951 property developers had begun to cast their eyes in the direction of the Oakland Stadium, and there even had been attempts to purchase the property that the racetrack was situated on. After all, it was a prime piece of real estate, with frontage on both East Fourteenth Street and Hesperian Boulevard.

East Fourteenth was already the main north/south arterial from metropolitan downtown Oakland leading to the southern expanses of Alameda County. Natural growth patterns of the East Bay area would indicate that the population would grow in a direction south of Oakland and San Leandro. Hesperian Blvd., at this point a secondary thoroughfare, would easily become a main route to all of the area through the quickly expanding San Lorenzo Village and points to the west and south of the city of Hayward.

Post War Boom

The post-war building boom had already arrived. Much of what had been rural truck-farm land of southern Alameda County was being bought up, and built over with much-needed housing for the new families who had relocated there during and after the war. Case in point: San Lorenzo Village, a scant two miles from the speedway, had begun building low-cost homes during 1944 while the war was still raging. The Bohannan Company, builder and developer of San Lorenzo, had convinced the government to ease wartime restrictions on building materials so that there would be a ready supply of housing for returning GIs. Hesperian Blvd, starting at East Fourteenth and 150th Avenue, continued south right through the middle of San Lorenzo Village.

It was no wonder that developers were eyeing the speedway property. It was perfectly situated for the building of a major shopping center to serve the many new residents who were beginning to pour into the area.

One of the first inklings that the racetrack might be in jeopardy appeared as several notices printed in a racing program for a big car race in June of 1953. A short article in that program announced the final race at the stadium for big cars and roadsters. In a July '53 program, a bold heading stated "The roar of the mighty Midgets will be heard for the last time at the Oakland Speedway today. It's the farewell performance of the Bay Cities Racing Association's racers."

A Commercial Center to Be Built

That same program announced that "a 500-lap stock car race is billed for August 2nd [1953] with work of tearing down the track to begin immediately afterwards." The *Oakland Tribune* of the previous day noted "The Championship Battle will be the finale at the Speedway, which changes ownership on Monday to make way for a commercial center."

That Sunday's *Tribune* announced "More than 30 of the west's top drivers will compete today in the 1953 National 500-lap Stock Car Race, the final race at the Oakland Speedway. The event will be the finale for the track which has been sold for a million dollar shopping center."

Apparently something happened with the immediate plans for a shopping center, because the *Tribune* of November 8, 1953 reported "A re-opening of the Oakland Stadium is announced, a Pacific Coast, Late Model Stock Car race to be held on the new, one-half mile dirt/asphalt track." Even though the August event had been announced as being the last, no one had seen evidence of the track being torn down.

Racing continued at the track all through the winter, and into the spring and summer of 1954 as if nothing out of the ordinary was about to happen.[1]

Bay-Fair Shopping Center Announced

And then, in a major article from the *Tribune* of August 26, 1954, came the block-buster news that, "Construction plans for the new $25,000,000 Bay-Fair shopping center, which will bring Macy's with a $6,000,000 department store to the Oakland area for the first time, were announced today."

The article stemmed from a press conference heralding the project's start. The paper went on to say, "The huge project got underway in the Ashland area, between Hayward and San Leandro at 154th Avenue and East 14th Street, with the start of demolition of the Oakland Speedway which stands on part of the shopping center site.

"The announcement of construction plans for the 48-acre regional project was made by the Capital Company, a subsidiary of Transamerica Corporation (Bank of America), Beckett and Federighi, an Oakland land developer, and Macy's California, a division of R.H. Macy Company, Inc. It was further stated that upon completion of the project in September of 1955, the center, which has won nationwide attention with its prize-winning design, is expected to serve some 350,000 shoppers within 15 minutes driving time of its site."

It's interesting to note that buried in the article was the statement that "Market research for Bay-Fair has been under way since 1951, and the center has been planned to handle estimated shopping demands of $35,000,000 annually by the year 1960." Really! It also was noted that the population of Alameda County in 1940 was 513,000, that by 1960 it was projected to be over 1,000,000 persons, and that most of that population would be within a few miles of the center site.

And then: nothing!

Track Idle in 1955

No races were held at the Oakland Stadium during 1955. In fact, no construction or destruction of any kind occurred during most of 1955. Finally, in the *Oakland Tribune* of August 27, 1955, came this short notice:

"A new one-mile auto speedway is being planned to replace the Oakland Speedway, now being torn down to make way for a $25,000,000 shopping center, Speedway operators Harry Schilling and A.J. McGrete said yesterday. They were considering three locations in the East Bay and expect the new track to be completed by April 1, [1956]."

It never came to pass.

Finally, in September 1955, an aerial photograph of the gen-

---

[1] Alan Ward, Sports Editor for the *Oakland Tribune* wrote, in part, on March 26, 1954: "During the past 2-3 years, Mack McGrete and Harry Schilling, operators of the Speedway were faced with momentary dispossession from the racing plant, which reportedly has been purchased as a site for a huge department store. Apparently the property deal is off, or at least delayed indefinitely. The promoters expect to be doing business at the same old stand not only this year, but in 1955 and 1956."

eral area revealed that, sure enough, some demolishing of the race track had taken place. The very sharp photo shows that the grandstands had been torn down; only the support pillars were left standing. It also shows that a bulldozer had made deep cuts across the pavement portions of the race track, that included the front and back straightaway as well as through the radius of the short, quarter-mile turn going through the infield. It appeared that the concrete portions of the high walls were still intact. Obviously, the cuts across the track surface had been done to make sure that no thrill-seeking night riders got onto the property to see if they might be able to recreate some past racing episodes. The end had finally come.

Macy's Grand Opening

On Wednesday, August 7, 1957, the *Oakland Tribune* ran full-page ads announcing the "Grand Opening" of Macy's $6,000,000 store, the anchor for the Bay-Fair shopping center. Ribbon-cutting ceremonies for the opening on Friday, August 9th were attended by "thousands of visitors and shoppers." In ceremonial remarks to the crowd it was noted that, "Once the site of the Oakland Automobile Racing Stadium, Bay Fair is to be the only dual-level shopping center in the entire West." It was also announced that by November eighty additional shops would open, making it one of the greatest shopping centers in the West.[2] Where once stood two famous auto race tracks, now stands a glorious monument to urban sprawl.

That's progress, I guess.

---

[2] On Wednesday, November 6, 1957, the *Oakland Tribune* announced that on the next day, Thursday, twenty-two more stores would open, to join Macy's, at the new $25,000,000 shopping center.

Oakland Tribune

August 27, 1955

A new one-mile speedway is being planned to replace the Oakland Speedway, now being torn down to make way for a $25,000,000 shopping center.

Speedway operators Harry Schilling and A.J. McGrete said yesterday, they were considering three locations in the East Bay and expect the new track to be completed by April 1 (1956).

This aerial photo was taken August 29, 1955. Destruction of the Speedway had already begun. Close examination of the grandstand area shows they have already been dismantled and only the piers are showing. Bulldozers have taken cuts across the front and back straightaways and through the rounded corner of the 1/4-mile portion of the track (the dark diagonal marks are cuts through the pavement into the dirt base). During 1954 both high-banked turns had been filled in with dirt, leveling the turns and leaving the straightaways paved. Not long after this photo was taken, the track was completely leveled for the new Bayfair Shopping Center.
(Bob Rushing Collection)

INDEX

Page numbers in **bold** indicate a photograph

A
Abreu, Jim vii
Acme Special 83
Adkins, Allen 101
Agabashian, Freddie 4, 58, 59, **61, 62, 64, 67, 84, 87, 90,** 91, 99, **104,** 165
Agajanian, J. C. 13, 39, 168
Alabam Café 2
Alameda Auto Wreckers 167
Alameda Naval Air Station 196
Alexander, Mel **162**
Alger, Jim **146, 161**
All-American Soap Box Derby 3, 145, 148
Allen, Abdo **92,** 164
Amans, Bill 61
Ameral, George **67**
American Automobile Association (AAA) 12, 13, 14, 38, 39, 46, 48, 49, 52, 54, 80, 107, 142
American Motorcycle Association (AMA) 3
American Racing Association (ARA) 12, 14, 24, 26, 29, 31, 37, 48, 51, 80, 81, 85, 99, 102, 108, 111, 115, 120, 129, 132, 134, 140, 168,
Amick, Bill **118**
Amick, George 99, **107, 109, 116**
Archer, David J. (Boots) v, vii, 88

Ascot Park (Gardena, CA) 168
Atkins, Dick 168

B
Baldwin, Marsh 26, 39
Barkhimer, Robert (Bob, "Barkie") vii, 58, **67,** 140, 164, 165, 166, 167
Barlest, Leo **170, 183**
Barnett, Ed **26, 32, 55**
Barron, Lamar **180**
Bartell, Harry 3
Baxter Stadium (Stockton, CA) 80, 166
Bay Area Rapid Transit (BART) 2
Bay Cities Racing Association (BCRA) 4, 13, 58, 59, 60, 62, 64, 73, 74, 84, 88, 89, 99, 102, 104, 107, 114, 133, 138, 140, 158, 164, 165, 166, 167, 168, 172, 177, 181, 185, 186, 188
Bay Cities Roadster Racing Association (BCRRA) 99, 138
Bay Meadows Raceway (San Mateo, CA) 81, 168
Bay-Fair (Bayfair) Shopping Center x, 189, 190, 192
Bayfair Shopping Plaza (San Leandro, CA) 2
BCRA, The First Fifty Years x, 138, 195
Beaver, Jack **169, 171**
Belfiore, Sammy vii
Belmont Stadium (Belmont, CA) 139

Bennett, Eddie **59, 83, 93, 94, 95, 96, 104, 107,** 114, 165, 166
Bennett, J. D. (a.k.a. Jim Lamport) vii, **114, 116, 143, 160**
Benoit, Al **20, 29, 41**
Berado, Vic 87
Betts, S. **173**
Bignotti, George 74, 76, 84, 87, 165, **181**
Birgnardello, Gino **157**
Blaylock, Stan **124**
Bloberger, Jim 141
Boggs, Wallace 3
Boyd, Johnny 59, **95**
Brenneman, Ken 80
Brooks, Stan 85
Brown, Woody 58, 59, **77, 92, 94, 95, 96,** 99, 100, 101, **104, 120,** 128, **134**
Brunner, Judge A. W. 3, **8**
Burke, Bob vii
Burke, Marvin **66, 77, 87,** 99, 100, 102, **104, 105, 107,** 114, 123, **131,** 134, 165
Burley, Mel 59, 70, 76, 86, 87
Burnaugh, Cecil **40, 48**
Busby, Floyd vii

C
Caldecott, Thomas 3
California State Railroad Museum (Sacramento, CA) 195

California Stock Car Racing Association (CSCRA) 102, 140, 165, 166, 167, 168, 172
Calistoga Speedway 196
Canadian Aces 174
Cancilla, Cos 70, 71
Cancilla, Tony 150
Carl Hungness Publishing (Speedway, IN) 6, 12
Carmody, Jack 25
Carrell Speedway (Gardena, CA) 24, 39
Carter, Dave 168
Carter, Dick 168
Carter, Duane 14, **38, 48**
Casale, Ernie 64
Caswell, Bob 100, **113**
Cavanagh, Frankie 58, 59
Central California Racing Association (CCRA) 139
Championship Auto Racing Team (CART) 142
Cheek, Tommy **70**
Chevrolet Motor Car Division (General Motors) 148
Chini, Jim vii
Chitwood, Joie (Auto Daredevils, Thrill Circus) 3, 174, 175
Clark, Sim 168
Clifford, Francis 3
Clovis Speedway (Clovis, CA) 196
Coates, Johnny **116**
Coelho family 2
Cole, Hal 13, **50, 80**

College of the Pacific (Stockton, CA) 80
Contra Costa Stadium (Pacheco, CA) 139
Conze Offy 14, 48
Cook, Jim vii
Corbin, Red 18
Costa, Gene **169, 171**
Cracknell, George 3
Crane, Bill Jr. 3
Curryer, Charles x, 2, 5, **8**, 12, 13, 18, 29, 37, 41, **48**, 58, **80, 81**, 88, 99, **111, 134**, 148, 168

D

Dana Photo (Berkeley, CA) 139
Danburg, George **156**
Dane, Lloyd 101, 113
Davies, Jim 139
Davis, Jack 166, 167
Dayton Speedway (Dayton, OH) 5, 142
Dean, Al 83
Distant Thunder x
Dobry Hal 16
Douglas, Grant 32, 33
Dudley, Gene **173**

E

Ed Sullivan Show 166, 173
Elisian, Ed **22, 87**, 99, **104**, 139, 141, **146, 150, 161, 162**
Emeryville Speedway (Emeryville, CA) 164
Erickson, Fred 59, **94, 95, 96**
Eschenburg, Rod vii
Evans, Everett 165

F

Faulkner, Walt 99, **107**, 114
Feehan, Bob 77, 166
Fernandez, Mel **107**

Figaro, Lou 100, 109, 111, **115, 116, 123**, 128
Figone, Lou 3
Flaherty, Jack **36**, 141
Flock, Fonty 100
Ford, Chuck **87, 183**
Fox, Jack C. 6, 12
Frame, Bob **37**
Frame, Fred 13, 37
France, Bill 167
Franks, Billy 5, **15**
Frey, Lemoine 139, 140, 141
Friday, Fred 58, 59, **61, 67, 72**, 79, 94, **95, 96**
Fry's Auto Wreckers (San Leandro, CA) 25, 34, 42
Ft. Wayne Speedway (Ft. Wayne, IN) 5

G

Gable, Clark 27, 68, **69**
Garabedian, Mike vii
Garner, Bob 3
Gaynor, Jack 49
Gemsa, Joe **23, 80, 125, 128**
George, Art 39
George, Elmer x, 60, 105, 139, 141, **147, 154, 157**
George, Tony 60, 141, 147
Gillson, Eric 20
Gleason, Sheriff H. P. 3, **8**
Glidewell, Floyd 25, **34, 42**
Gonzel, Lenny 77
Gotelli, Vic 61
Gregory, Ben 100, 101, **102, 112, 118**, 125, 128, 134
Gubanski, Walt vii
Guisti, Joe **180**

H

Hagemann, Jack 154
Hansen, Ted 165
Harder, Judge Jacob 3, **8**

Harley Davidson Motorcycle Co. 80
Harper, Roland vii
Hawks, Sam **51**, 139, 140, **151, 154**
Hayward Chamber of Commerce (Hayward, CA) 3
Heath, Allen 100
Heath, Jim **118, 134, 136**
Hennig, Rudy 92
Hiatt, Ray vii
Hill, Herb **146, 161**
Hill, Jerry 140
Hoffman, Dan 3
Holt, Jimmy 59, **94, 95, 96**
Holtkamp, Norm 58, 59, **67**
Hunefeld, Billy 166
Hopkins, George **171**
Hoyt, Jerry 5
Hubbard Auto Parts (Cherryland, CA) 152
Hubbard, Ben **158**
Hubbard, Dick 152
Hubbard, Meeks 3
Hughes Stadium (Sacramento, CA) 139, 166
Humphers, Lee **172**, 178

I

Illustrated Speedway News 164
Indianapolis Motor Speedway (Indianapolis, IN) 59, 60, 141, 147, 181
Indianapolis Racing League (IRL) 60, 142, 147

J

Jack Maurer Offy 26
James, Joe x, 14
James, Walt **30, 104, 136**
Janssen, George 3, **8**
Johnston, Lyle **85**
Journal of the Emeryville Historical Society 195
K.O. Special 52, 56

K

Kaiser-Frazer Motor Company 100
Kelleher, Bob 141
Kelleher, Bud 139
Key (Keys, Keyes), Johnny 105, 139, **180**
Kincade, Joyce **26**
Klann, John E. vii
Kolb, Don 139, 155
Kurtis-Kraft Midget: A Genealogy of Speed x
Kurtis-Kraft 164

L

Lamport, Jim (a.k.a. J.D. Bennett) vii, **114, 143, 160**
Lattell, Norm 60
Lawlor, Charlie 60
Lazy J Speedway (Sacramento, CA) 139
Lee, Dave **36**
Lester, Tommy ("Lucky Les") **176**
Letner, Danny 101, **107**, 113
Levrett, Bayliss vii, 13, 17, **24**, 25, **26, 40, 44, 53, 81, 108**
Levrett, John 25
Life Magazine 166, 173
Linden, Andy 5, 14, **38**, 100, 108, 117, 132
Linn, William E. (Bill) x, 2, 3, 5, **8**, 58
Livingston, Bert **132**
Lockhart, Ed 140
Lodi Grape Bowl (Lodi, CA) 80, 166
London, Jack 60, 64, 87, 165
Lopez, Angel 174
Low, Betty 25
Low, Lenny vii, 13, **16, 17**, 24, **25, 34, 48**

M

Machin, Bob vii, 60, 61, 139, 140, 141, **158**
Macy's (R.H. Macy Co., Inc.) 189, 190
Mahalis, George 141
Maher, Bill 166, 167, **173, 186**
Malloy Offy 14, 39
Malloy, Emmett 46
Mantz, Johnny 13, 14, **38, 39**, 99, 100
Marcoe, Bob **152**
Massa, Jimmy 66, **93**, 166
Mathews, Marshall 20
Matteucci, Gus 60
McDonald, Bill vii
McDonald, Ted **22**
McGrath, Jack 48
McGreevy, Mike **70, 91**, 165, **173**
McGrete, A. J. ("Mack") 167, 189, 191
McGriff, Hershel 101, **104**, 105, **106**, 112, **113, 119, 122, 126**, 127, **134**
Mehalis, George **36, 42**
Menges, Pat vii
Menser, Jack **27**
Merkler Machine Works (Ft. Wayne, IN) 24
Metro-Goldwyn-Mayer 68
Meyer, Dick **122, 128**
Meyer-Drake Engineering Corp.(Los Angeles, CA) 38
Meyers, Dick 100
Miller, Ernie **36, 51**
Millet, Jeff vii
Modesto 99 Speedway (Modesto, CA) 139
Montgomery, Arlene vii
Montgomery, Bill vii, x
Montgomery, Jim vii
Morales Offy 14

Morales, Alex 43
Morrow, Tommy 60, 61
Motter, Earl 13, 27, 59, 60, 61, **76, 77, 78, 82, 86, 89, 155**, 197
Motter, Mary Jane vii, 197
Motter, Rob vii
Motter, Tom x, 138, **197**
Mount, Chuck **169**

N

Napa County Fair Speedway (Calistoga, CA) 141
National Association of Stock Car Auto Racing (NASCAR) 99, 101, 103, 111, 118, 121, 126, 142, 167
National Speed Sport News 164
Niday, Cal 14
Normi, Ed 58, 59, **61**, 62, **67, 74, 75**, 101, 166, **186**
Northern Auto Racing Club (NARC) 81, 168
Northern California Roadster Racing Association (NCRRA) 138, 139

O

Oakland Airport (Oakland, CA) 2
Oakland Drive-In (San Leandro, CA) ix
Oakland Post Enquirer (Oakland, CA) 139, 148
Oakland Racing Association (ORA) 167, 168
Oakland Speedway (San Leandro, CA) 2, 80
Oakland Tribune (Oakland, CA) 7, 8, 9, 68, 80, 88, 100, 140, 141, 166, 167, 173, 185, 186, 188, 189, 190, 191
Official BCRA 1980 Yearbook x
Olson, Bud **169, 171, 183**
Ornellas, Tommy **170, 183**

Oroville Speedway (Oroville, CA) 141
Orr, Karl 14, 22, 38, 39, 52

P

Pacheco, George 139, **162**
Pagan, Marian 101
Palmer, Clyde 101, 141, **170**
Panch, Marvin 100, 101, **107, 111,** **113, 122, 127**, 128, **173, 180**
Papina, Al **90**
Parsons, Johnnie **54**
Peters, Cliff **157**
Peterson, Tex 26
Petruzzi, Vince 83
Petschaver, Ed **85**
Petty, Lee 101, **103, 126**
Petty, Richard 101
Phillips, Frank **108, 111**
Piper, Jerry 58, 59, 165
Pombo, Al **172, 184**
Pries, Fred vii
Purdy, Hugh **178**

R

Radbruch, Don vii, 140, 141
Radigonda, Rich vii, **198**
Rajo Jack (Jack DeSoto) **21, 28**
Ramage, Bob 61
Rathmann, Dick 100, 101, 103, 118, 126
Reed, Jim 4, 38, **111**
Reed, Randy vii
Reed, Russ vii, 68, 109, 153, 157, 166, 173, 186
Reese, Dickie 165, **179**
Richards, Chet **158**
Richter, Roy 64
Rickman, Eric 139
Rigsby, Jim 14, **43**
Roadster Racing Incorporated (RRI) 139, 158, 161

Roaring Roadsters 140
Roberts, Cliff 165, 166, 167, **173, 180, 182**
Roletto, Joe **36**
Rose, Bud 5, 13, **19**, 24, **27, 40, 45, 56**, 68, **69**, 99, 105, **109, 114, 135**
Rossi, Don **36**
Rowell, George 162
Rushing, Bob vii, 156, 165, **177**
Ruttman, Troy x, 13, 14, **39, 43, 46, 54**, 99, 139, 141
Ryan, Billy **71**

S

Sacramento Stadium (Hughes Stadium, Sacramento, CA) 80
Salem Speedway (Salem, IN) 5, 142
Salinas Speedway (Salinas, CA) 139
Sample, Tony **135**
San Jose Speedway (San Jose, CA) 139, 140, 165
Sanchez, C. **173**
Sanders, Ben 162
Santa Rosa Speedway (Santa Rosa, CA) 139
Santos, Frank **181**
Schellinger, Bob 141
Schilling, Harry 77, 92, 166, 167, 189, 191
Scofield, Alice vii
Scott, Bob 14, **54**
Scott, Dick **148, 149**
Scott, Don vii, **148, 149**
Sennett, Bud (Scorchy) 14, **22**, 39, 100
Sheffler, Bill 5, 13, **27**, 40, **55**, 59
Shellenger, Bob **157**
Sheppard, Charles **108**
Shirley, Bob 147, 154
Silva, Bob vii
Simpson, Bob **180**
Slinker, Al 139, **146, 161**

Slonaker, Al 88
Smith, Don 61, 62, **67**
Smith, Ed 83
Smith, Jack 167
Smith, Johnny 58, 59, **61, 67, 92, 104, 108**, 165, 178, **181**
Soares, Johnny 59, 60, **67, 75, 91**, 99, 100, 101, **102, 104, 105, 106, 108**, 110, 111, **112, 116, 117**, 120, **128, 131, 134, 135**, 165, 166, **181**
Speedo-Electric Special 72
Speedway Age Magazine 4
Stadium Auto Movie (San Leandro, CA) ix
Stanford University (Palo Alto, CA) 5
Stanwyck, Barbara 68
Staver, Jack vii, **79**
Steinbroner, Fred **105, 109, 116**
Stern, Les **180**
Stockton 99 Speedway (Stockton, CA) 139
Sutherland, Gordy **186**
Sweikert, Bob x, 13, 14, 38, 39, **52, 56**, 59, 60, **76, 78, 89**, 99, **102, 104, 109, 116**, 139, 141

T

Terra, Larry **94**, 59, 139, **150**
Tessien, Gene 60, **83**, 139, **150, 154**
The History of the Oakland Speedway (1931-1941) 195
The History of the Oakland Stadium (1946-1955) x, 195
The Illustrated History of Sprint Car Racing 12
Theal, Ducky 3
Thomas, Art vii
Thompson, F. **173**
Ticonderoga 196
To Please a Lady 68
Tracy High School (Tracy, CA) 80

Transamerica Corp. (Bank of America) 189
Trueblood, Gerald vii
Tucker, Archie **184**

U

United Racing Association (URA) 88
United States Auto Club (USAC) 107, 140, 158
Uptown Motors (Berkeley, CA) 51
Urton, Ken vii, **176**

V

Valenti, Joe (Jumpin') **133, 150, 173, 180**
Vallejo Speedway (Vallejo, CA) 167, 168
Veith, Bob 14, 60, 99, **104**, 139, 141, **144**
Vermiel, Al **48**
Vermiel, Louie 48
Vermiel, Stan 48
Viglienzone, Herk 151
Viglienzone, Randy vii
Vukovich, Bill 101, 141
Vukovich, Eli 83, 101, 141

W

Walling, Claude **108, 129**
Walsh, Dee vii
Walters, Lucky 174
Ward, Alan 80, 189
Ward, Bill 174
Ward, Roger 99, **117**
Watkins, Tom **169**
Watts, Art **118**
Weeks, Foster 2, 7
Weinberg, Danny **116**
Wells, Curly **67**
Wendt, Eddie **62, 67**

West Capitol Speedway (West Sacramento, CA) 196
West Coast Racing Association (WCRA) 140, 141, 166, 167
West, Mel 178
Western Pacific Railroad 2
Western Racing Association (WRA) 22, 26, 99, 110, 114, 116, 117, 123, 128, 135
Whitmer, Buck **27, 33, 45, 67, 85**
Wiebe, Walter vii
Wilhelm, Bob **169**
Williams, Bill **180**
Williamson, Bud 165
Willis, Keith 166, 167, **173, 180**
Wilson, Dempsey 14, **49**
Winchester Speedway (Winchester, IN) 5, 142
Woolman, Harry 174
Wright, Jerry **183**

Z

Zanolini, Rod **173**, 178

The Author

Tom Motter is a racing historian in the truest sense. His lifelong interest in West Coast auto racing has brought him in contact with many aspects of the sport: its race tracks, the drivers, the cars, and the fans. His memorabilia collection, acquired since the age of ten, fills most of the space in his Sacramento home that he shares with his wife, Mary Jane. His uncle Earl Motter was a midget, sprint car, and Indy-Championship car driver in the 40s and 50s, and to say that Uncle Earl was a major influence on Tom's life would be an understatement.

Tom's interest in midget racing began in 1946, the same year that Uncle Earl came back from World War II and resumed his midget racing career in the San Francisco Bay Area. The then brand-new Oakland Stadium, in San Leandro, was only a few miles from Tom's childhood residence, and it was there that he saw his first midget race. This lifelong interest in midget racing brought about the writing of his first book, *BCRA, The First 50 Years*, the official history of the Bay Cities Racing Association, published in 1990.

In 1987 he formed the Vintage Division as a part of BCRA. From 1991 until 1995 Tom served on the Board of Directors of that organization, and served as its Director of Racing in 1993 and '94. Since 1984 Tom has written numerous articles on the history of midget racing in northern California. These articles have appeared in national magazines as well as in racing programs throughout northern California. Early in 1999 he wrote the feature article entitled "Early Day Midget Racing," published in the *Journal of the Emeryville Historical Society* (Volume X, Number 1, spring 1999).

His next two books, published in 2001, *The History of the Oakland Speedway (1931-1941)*, and *The History of the Oakland Stadium (1946-1955)* are volumes one and two of a projected series of five that will cover the history of northern California race tracks, now long gone.

When not busy writing about auto racing, Tom volunteers his time at the California State Railroad Museum in Sacramento as a docent and tour guide, recounting the history of railroads in the western United States.

The Artist

The cover art was done by Rich Radigonda, who resides in the quaint town of Benicia, California. When not working on his newly-acquired duck club Rich spends his time painting from his second story studio overlooking the famed Carquinez Straits.

Born and raised in San Francisco, his interest in art began at the age of five when he began drawing pictures of the World War II airplanes that he saw flying over the city heading for the Alameda Naval Air Station. His interest in aircraft led to a stint in the Navy, serving aboard the aircraft carrier *Ticonderoga* in the late 1950s. There, he made many sketches of flight deck action and painted cartoons and nose art on the fighter planes.

In the early 1960s Rich sponsored a super-modified race car and performed all of the mechanical work on the car. The car won the 1963 northern California championship, and held records at tracks such as West Capitol, Clovis, and Calistoga.

Next came collecting antique duck decoys, and eventually Rich took to hand-carving his own decoys. He then found an interest in photographing wildlife, which led to painting waterfowl on canvas. In 1980 Rich began oil painting in earnest, and he soon became good enough to enter the Duck Stamp painting competitions. In 1993, one of Rich's paintings placed second in a "California Duck Stamp" competition.

The last few years have found Rich creating paintings of World War II aircraft, as well as keeping up with his interest in waterfowl. His renewed interest in auto racing brought about the wonderful oil paintings selected as cover art on the two historical volumes on the Oakland Speedway/Oakland Stadium, volumes one and two in the Tracks of the West series.